Gulf-Mirage

1967 to 1982

Other great books from Veloce –

Rally Giants Series
Audi Quattro (Robson)
Austin Healey 100-6 & 3000 (Robson)
Fiat 131 Abarth (Robson)
Ford Escort MkI (Robson)
Ford Escort RS1800 (Robson)
Ford Escort RS Cosworth & World Rally Car (Robson)
Ford Escort RS1800 (Robson)
Lancia Delta 4WD/Integrale (Robson)
Lancia Stratos (Robson)
Mini Cooper/Mini Cooper S (Robson)
Peugeot 205 T16 (Robson)
Saab 96 & V4 (Robson)
Subaru Impreza (Robson)
Toyota Celica GT4 (Robson)

WSC Giants
Audi R8 (Wagstaff)
Ferrari 312P & 312PB (Collins & McDonough)
Ferrari 333 SP (O'Neil)
Gulf-Mirage 1967 to 1982 (McDonough)
Matra Sports Cars – MS620, 630, 650, 660 & 670 – 1966 to 1974 (McDonough)

General
1½-litre GP Racing 1961-1965 (Whitelock)
AC Two-litre Saloons & Buckland Sportscars (Archibald)
Alfa Romeo 155/156/147 Competition Touring Cars (Collins)
Alfa Romeo Giulia Coupé GT & GTA (Tipler)
Alfa Romeo Montreal – The dream car that came true (Taylor)
Alfa Romeo Montreal – The Essential Companion (Classic Reprint of 500 copies) (Taylor)
Alfa Tipo 33 (McDonough & Collins)
Alpine & Renault – The Development of the Revolutionary Turbo F1 Car 1968 to 1979 (Smith)
Alpine & Renault – The Sports Prototypes 1963 to 1969 (Smith)
1978 (Smith)
Anatomy of the Classic Mini (Huthert & Ely)
Anatomy of the Works Minis (Moylan)
Armstrong-Siddeley (Smith)
Autodrome (Collins & Ireland)
Bahamas Speed Weeks, The (O'Neil)
Bentley Continental, Corniche and Azure (Bennett)
Bentley MkVI, Rolls-Royce Silver Wraith, Dawn & Cloud/Bentley R & S-Series (Nutland)
Bluebird CN7 (Stevens)
BMC Competitions Department Secrets (Turner, Chambers & Browning)
BMW 5-Series (Cranswick)
BMW Classic 5 Series 1972 to 2003 (Cranswick)
BMW – The Power of M (Vivian)
BRM – A Mechanic's Tale (Salmon)
BRM V16 (Ludvigsen)
Bugatti – The 8-cylinder Touring Cars 1920-34 (Price & Arbey)
Bugatti Type 40 (Price)
Bugatti 46/50 Updated Edition (Price & Arbey)
Bugatti T44 & T49 (Price & Arbey)
Bugatti 57 2nd Edition (Price)
Bugatti Type 57 Grand Prix – A Celebration (Tomlinson)
Carrera Panamericana, La (Tipler)
Chrysler 300 – America's Most Powerful Car 2nd Edition (Ackerson)
Chrysler PT Cruiser (Ackerson)
Citroën DS (Bobbitt)
Classic British Car Electrical Systems (Astley)
Cobra – The Real Thing! (Legate)
Competition Car Aerodynamics 3rd Edition (McBeath)
Competition Car Composites A Practical Handbook

(Revised 2nd Edition) (McBeath)
Concept Cars, How to illustrate and design – New 2nd Edition (Dewey)
Cortina – Ford's Bestseller (Robson)
Cosworth – The Search for Power (6th edition) (Robson)
Coventry Climax Racing Engines (Hammill)
Daily Mirror 1970 World Cup Rally 40, The (Robson)
Daimler SP250 New Edition (Long)
Datsun Fairlady Roadster to 280ZX – The Z-Car Story (Long)
Dino – The V6 Ferrari (Long)
Dodge Challenger & Plymouth Barracuda (Grist)
Dodge Charger – Enduring Thunder (Ackerson)
Dodge Dynamite! (Grist)
Ferrari 288 GTO, The Book of the (Sackey)
Ferrari 333 SP (O'Neil)
Fiat & Abarth 124 Spider & Coupé (Tipler)
Fiat & Abarth 500 & 600 – 2nd Edition (Bobbitt)
Fiats, Great Small (Ward)
Ford Cleveland 335-Series V8 engine 1970 to 1982 – The Essential Source Book (Hammill)
Ford F100/F150 Pick-up 1948-1996 (Ackerson)
Ford F150 Pick-up 1997-2005 (Ackerson)
Ford Focus WRC (Robson)
Ford GT – Then, and Now (Streather)
Ford GT40 (Legate)
Ford Midsize Muscle – Fairlane, Torino & Ranchero (Cranswick)
Ford Model Y (Roberts)
Ford Small Block V8 Racing Engines 1962-1970 – The Essential Source Book (Hammill)
Ford Thunderbird From 1954, The Book of the (Long)
Formula One – The Real Score? (Harvey)
Formula 5000 Motor Racing, Back then ... and back now (Lawson)
Forza Minardi! (Vigar)
France: the essential guide for car enthusiasts – 200 things for the car enthusiast to see and do (Parish)
Grand Prix Ford – DFV-powered Formula 1 Cars (Robson)
GT – The World's Best GT Cars 1953-73 (Dawson)
Hillclimbing & Sprinting – The Essential Manual (Short & Wilkinson)
Honda NSX (Long)
Inside the Rolls-Royce & Bentley Styling Department – 1971 to 2001 (Pitcher)
Intermeccanica – The Story of the Prancing Bull (McCredie & Reisner)
Jaguar, The Rise of (Price)
Jaguar XJ 220 – The Inside Story (Moreton)
Jaguar XJ-S, The Book of the (Long)
Jeep CJ (Ackerson)
Jeep Wrangler (Ackerson)
The Jowett Jupiter – The car that leaped to fame (Nankivell)
Karmann-Ghia Coupé & Convertible (Bobbitt)
Kris Meeke – Intercontinental Rally Challenge Champion (McBride)
Lamborghini Miura Bible, The (Sackey)
Lamborghini Urraco, The Book of the (Landsem)
Lancia 037 (Collins)
Lancia Delta HF Integrale (Blaettel & Wagner)
Land Rover Series III Reborn (Porter)
Land Rover, The Half-ton Military (Cook)
Lea-Francis Story, The (Price)
Le Mans Panoramic (Ireland)
Lexus Story, The (Long)
Lola – The Illustrated History (1957-1977) (Starkey)
Lola – All the Sports Racing & Single-seater Racing Cars 1978-1997 (Starkey)

Lola T70 – The Racing History & Individual Chassis Record – 4th Edition (Starkey)
Lotus 18 Colin Chapman's U-turn (Whitelock)
Lotus 49 (Oliver)
Maserati 250F In Focus (Pritchard)
Mazda MX-5/Miata 1.6 Enthusiast's Workshop Manual (Grainger & Shoemark)
Mazda MX-5/Miata 1.8 Enthusiast's Workshop Manual (Grainger & Shoemark)
Mazda MX-5 Miata, The book of the – The 'Mk1' NA-series 1988 to 1997 (Long)
Mazda MX-5 Miata Roadster (Long)
Mazda Rotary-engined Cars (Cranswick)
Maximum Mini (Booij)
Meet the English (Bowie)
Mercedes-Benz SL – R230 series 2001 to 2011 (Long)
Mercedes-Benz SL – W113-series 1963-1971 (Long)
Mercedes-Benz SL & SLC – 107-series 1971-1989 (Long)
Mercedes-Benz SLK – R170 series 1996-2004 (Long)
Mercedes-Benz SLK – R171 series 2004-2011 (Long)
Mercedes-Benz W123-series – All models 1976 to 1986 (Long)
Mercedes G-Wagen (Long)
MGA (Price Williams)
MGB & MGB GT– Expert Guide (Auto-doc Series) (Williams)
MGB Electrical Systems Updated & Revised Edition (Astley)
Mini Cooper – The Real Thing! (Tipler)
Mini Minor to Asia Minor (West)
Mitsubishi Lancer Evo, The Road Car & WRC Story (Long)
Montlhéry, The Story of the Paris Autodrome (Boddy)
Morgan Maverick (Lawrence)
Morgan 3 Wheeler – back to the future!, The (Dron)
Morris Minor, 60 Years on the Road (Newell)
Motor Racing – The Pursuit of Victory 1930-1962 (Carter)
Motor Racing – The Pursuit of Victory 1963-1972 (Wyatt/Sears)
Motor Racing Heroes – The Stories of 100 Greats (Newman)
Motorsport In colour, 1950s (Wainwright)
N.A.R.T. – A concise history of the North American Racing Team 1957 to 1983 (O'Neil)
Nissan 300ZX & 350Z – The Z-Car Story (Long)
Nissan GT-R Supercar: Born to race (Gorodji)
Northeast American Sports Car Races 1950-1959 (O'Neil)
Pontiac Firebird – New 3rd Edition (Cranswick)
Porsche Boxster (Long)
Porsche 356 (2nd Edition) (Long)
Porsche 908 (Födisch, Neßhöver, Roßbach, Schwarz & Roßbach)
Porsche 911 Carrera – The Last of the Evolution (Corlett)
Porsche 911R, RS & RSR, 4th Edition (Starkey)
Porsche 911, The Book of the (Long)
Porsche 911 – The Definitive History 2004-2012 (Long)
Porsche – The Racing 914s (Long)
Porsche 911SC 'Super Carrera' – The Essential Companion (Streather)
Porsche 914 & 914-6: The Definitive History of the Road & Competition Cars (Long)
Porsche 924 (Long)
The Porsche 924 Carreras – evolution to excellence (Smith)
Porsche 928 (Long)
Porsche 944 (Long)
Porsche 964, 993 & 996 Data Plate Code Breaker (Streather)

Porsche 993 'King Of Porsche' – The Essential Companion (Streather)
Porsche 996 'Supreme Porsche' – The Essential Companion (Streather)
Porsche 997 2004-2012 – Porsche Excellence (Streather)
Porsche Racing Cars – 1953 to 1975 (Long)
Porsche Racing Cars – 1976 to 2005 (Long)
Porsche – The Rally Story (Meredith)
Porsche: Three Generations of Genius (Meredith)
Preston Tucker & Others (Linde)
RAC Rally Action! (Gardiner)
Rallye Sport Fords: The Inside Story (Moreton)
Rolls-Royce Silver Shadow/Bentley T Series Corniche & Camargue – Revised & Enlarged Edition (Bobbitt)
Rolls-Royce Silver Spirit, Silver Spur & Bentley Mulsanne 2nd Edition (Bobbitt)
Rootes Cars of the 50s, 60s & 70s – Hillman, Humber, Singer, Sunbeam & Talbot (Rowe)
Rover P4 (Bobbitt)
Runways & Racers (O'Neil)
RX-7 – Mazda's Rotary Engine Sportscar (Updated & Revised New Edition) (Long)
Singer Story: Cars, Commercial Vehicles, Bicycles & Motorcycle (Atkinson)
Sleeping Beauties USA – abandoned classic cars & trucks (Marek)
SM – Citroën's Maserati-engined Supercar (Long & Claverol)
Standard Motor Company, The Book of the (Robson)
Subaru Impreza: The Road Car And WRC Story (Long)
Supercar, How to Build your own (Thompson)
Tatra – The Legacy of Hans Ledwinka, Updated & Enlarged Collector's Edition of 1500 copies (Margolius & Henry)
To Boldly Go – twenty six vehicle designs that dared to be different (Hull)
Toyota Celica & Supra, The Book of Toyota's Sports Coupés (Long)
Toyota MR2 Coupés & Spyders (Long)
Triumph TR6 (Kimberley)
Two Summers – The Mercedes-Benz W196R Racing Car (Ackerson)
TWR Story, The – Group A (Hughes & Scott)
Unraced (Collins)
Volkswagen Bus Book, The (Bobbitt)
Volkswagen Bus or Van to Camper, How to Convert (Porter)
Volkswagens of the World (Glen)
VW Beetle Cabriolet – The full story of the convertible Beetle (Bobbitt)
VW Beetle – The Car of the 20th Century (Copping)
VW Bus – 40 Years of Splitties, Bays & Wedges (Copping)
VW Bus Book, The (Bobbitt)
VW Golf: Five Generations of Fun (Copping & Cservenka)
VW – The Air-cooled Era (Copping)
VW T5 Camper Conversion Manual (Porter)
VW Campers (Copping)
Volkswagen Type 3, The book of the – Concept, Design, International Production Models & Development (Glen)
Volvo Estate, The (Hollebone)
You & Your Jaguar XK8/XKR – Buying, Enjoying, Maintaining, Modifying – New Edition (Thorley)
Wolseley Cars 1948 to 1975 (Rowe)
Works Minis, The Last (Purves & Brenchley)
Works Rally Mechanic (Moylan)

www.veloce.co.uk

Velocce's other imprints:

First published in February 2012 by Veloce Publishing Limited, Veloce House, Parkway Farm Business Park, Middle Farm Way, Poundbury, Dorchester DT1 3AR, England. Fax 01305 250479 / e-mail info@veloce.co.uk / web www.veloce.co.uk or www.velocebooks.com. Reprinted July 2017. ISBN: 978-1-787111-75-2; UPC: 6-36847-01175-8.
Typesetting, design and page make-up all by Veloce Publishing Ltd on Apple Mac. Printed and bound by CPI Group (UK) Ltd, Croydon, CR0 4YY.

Veloce *Classic Reprint* Series

Gulf-Mirage

1967 to 1982

WSC GIANTS™

Ed McDonough • Foreword by Vern Schuppan

VELOCE

Contents

DEDICATION: This book is dedicated to the memory of John Wyer and all the JWA/GULF/GRR staff who left behind such a marvellous racing legacy.

Foreword
by Vern Schuppan

My first contact with the JW team came in 1969 after I'd arrived in the UK from Australia, and was racing in Formula Ford. The team had produced a Formula Ford, so I went along to Slough for a chat with John Horsman. Nothing came about in relation to Formula Ford, and in fact I didn't have further contact with JW until 1973, after I'd signed with BRM.

I was at Brands Hatch for the Race of Champions and qualified at the front with Beltoise and Lauda in the other BRM P160s, ahead of Jody Scheckter. During that race, John Watson crashed and broke his leg, so on Monday morning John Horsman phoned me and asked if I could drive for the JW-Gulf team until Watson had recovered. The first race was at Vallelunga where I was driving with Mike Hailwood and the engine tightened up. Following this, Mike and I got a fifth place at Dijon, didn't finish at Monza, and then had that great race at Spa for JW in 1973, where the Mirage cars were first and second. That was a special occasion. I had flown directly from Japan to Brussels for the Spa race, and when I arrived at the circuit John Horsman was saying, "... c'mon, c'mon, we've been waiting for you," and I got into my overalls and straight into the car. That was my first time at Spa, and I found it such an amazing and exhilarating track, probably the most amazing place I had ever been.

The Mirage was very good at Spa, and on other fast circuits. Spa was a place where you could drive that car flat, or very close to it, on most corners. It was still the early days of my racing career and it was so great to be doing what I was doing. Signing for BRM had been a turning point – I was to get an F1 test, and the test turned out to be going

Vern Schuppan. (Courtesy Mike Jiggle)

straight into a race. My career had moved very quickly from 1970 and a £900 Alexis, to Tony Macon asking me to drive one of his cars, then into Atlantic to BRM in 1972, and then in 1973 to F1 with BRM, with fifth and the fourth

Vern Schuppan and the author at their first meeting at Brands Hatch Race in 1973. (Courtesy K Randall)

in the two non-championships that year, and I was in one of the best sports car teams as well with Mirage. I thought I had cracked it! It was important that I had the Mirage drive when Lauda took my drive at BRM or I would have had nothing.

In 1974 I came back to the JW team and raced at the Nürburgring. As I drove by the pits, the steering column broke away from the dashboard, which meant I had a whole lap to drive with the thing floating around. You could still steer the car but it wasn't attached to anything. I came behind the pits as the track does at Nürburgring, and saw they had put out the 'Faster' sign – I thought this was going to be a horrific lap because I didn't know exactly what

had broken. The team wired the whole steering assembly back onto the dashboard and we managed to finish the race. Before the race, I'd been around the Nürburgring with Derek Bell in a road car and he'd said, 'It's flat here and here … ' So after the race I said to him, 'You're a brave bastard – there was no way I could go flat there,' and he said, 'Oh no, I wasn't serious.'

Then in 1975 at Le Mans we came first and third. To make the DFV engine last for 24 hours in both cars was very special. No one really expected the engines to last that long. In 1976 when I drove with Derek, we were having trouble restarting the engine, and I remember having to slip the clutch to keep it going out of the hairpin, because the revs dropped so low. I was very lucky to have been with the JW team when it did so well in those races. John Wyer and John Horsman always drummed into us that we must stick to the designated lap times, and that we must not come into the pits unless it was essential. You could look back and see that Wyer was able to predict just how many laps we had to do to win. Being in the team helped to establish me at Le Mans, where I finally had quite a good record of success, winning for Porsche in 1983, and driving there right up to 1990.

I learned a lot along the way. We did a lot of testing, and there was a lot of gin rummy which I had to learn, playing with Tottie Wyer. I knew I had arrived then! There were many good moments … driving at Spa and the team result there … and driving with Mike Hailwood. That was the year he sat on the fuel filler and had to have water thrown over his backside. That lost us time and we had to drive really hard to make it up, and had the one-two result – very memorable. There were good people in the team, and it was a very important time for me and my career.

Vern Schuppan

Introduction

The Mirage story is, in some ways, a rather complex one, in that the Mirage was not developed consistently year by year, as had been the case with Ferrari, Matra and Alfa Romeo in the late 1960s and early to mid-1970s. The Mirage was born from Ford and of necessity, and it took some time to establish itself as a marque in its own right. Like Ferrari, Matra and Alfa Romeo, it eventually became a front runner in the World Sports Car Championship, with notable victories and exciting performances from exceptional drivers.

The Mirage was largely the product of the work of two men who had a lasting impact on motor racing. One was rather better known than the other, but the second had a much longer connection with the racing Mirages than the former.

John Wyer had been the Competition Manager for Aston Martin Lagonda Ltd, and then General Manager of the company. In 1958, a young John Horsman had a job interview with Wyer, and was offered an apprentice position with the company. Horsman then worked very closely with Wyer in the later years of the Aston Martin racing programme, which was wound up at the end of 1963. Wyer then famously joined Ford to sort out the Ford GT40 for international sports car racing. Horsman went back to education at the end of 1963, but he accepted an invitation to join Wyer as his assistant at JW when he had completed his studies at London's LSE in June 1964. The pair were to work closely together for many years to come, and to remain friends even longer, Wyer eventually following Horsman out to Arizona to live.

Wyer and Horsman were based at the Yeovil Road

A portrait of the sometimes deceptively serious-looking John Wyer. (Courtesy Ford)

former headquarters of Lola Cars in Slough, working in the team Ford had put together in 1963. Eric Broadley was assigned there to turn the Lola GT (which had run

John Horsman in the midst of the action. David Yorke is on his right as he supervises work at Daytona. (Courtesy Lou Galanos)

at Le Mans in 1963) into the Ford GT40. Many Lola and former Aston Martin staff were engaged in this project. The Ford-funded GT40 was unsuccessful at Le Mans in 1964, and failed again at Reims just days later. Ford then set up its own project, Ford Advanced Vehicles, to have more control over the GT40 development. After the failure at Reims, Broadley left Ford politics behind, taking his staff and some of the ex-Aston people with him. English engineer Len Bailey, who had been working for Ford in the USA, and then came to Slough as part of the GT40 project, remained after the split with Broadley. Horsman became the engineer responsible for development, preparation and racing at Slough, and the JW/FAV force really began to take off.

The next two years witnessed a serious advance in sports car racing, and the continuation of Ford politics in motorsport. Though FAV had the contract to build 100 GT40s, later reduced to 50, much of Ford's racing became the responsibility of Carroll Shelby in the USA, who had joined Ford as a partner in 1965. FAV became rather less important to Ford, entering few races but doing virtually all the development work. In addition, American Ford engineer Roy Lunn had encouraged Ford to focus on a new car, the X-car – a NASCAR-engined chassis based on the GT40, which became the Ford MkII. This took place while FAV was still developing the GT40. When Ford lost at Le Mans in 1965, the FAV programme was cancelled, and then re-instated two weeks later under pressure from Wyer. In 1966 FAV was relegated to providing support for customer road and race cars. However, though Ford Shelby cars won Le Mans that year, FAV-supported cars won the World Sports Car Championship. Ford announced that the GT40 build programme would end that autumn, and the very last car was delivered just before Christmas 1966.

John Wyer purchased the assets of FAV in March 1966 as well as an agreement to continue to build and sell Ford GT40s. On January 1, 1967, the FAV sign was replaced by one which read JW Automotive Engineering Ltd, and the directors of this new company were Wyer, Horsman, and John Willment who provided financial investment.

Significantly, Gulf Oil Corporation executive Grady Davis had spoken to John Wyer in March 1966 and ordered a GT40 for himself, which was delivered in April, and he was very impressed with the car. The link with Davis and Gulf would mark a turning point for Wyer and Horsman. When Wyer was winding up the arrangements with Ford towards the end of 1966, he visited Gulf Oil headquarters. Gulf Oil Racing was subsequently created and Wyer's operation would have generous finance for the future. Though it did not yet have a name, the Mirage programme was under way.

Acknowledgements

Writing a book on Mirage has been a trip into my own past, rather like that experienced with the Ferrari 312P and Matra books, though with some distinct differences. In retrospect I was very fortunate to be 'on the scene' at one of the strongest periods in sports car racing.

I never owned one of the Ferraris or Matras, but I did have a Mirage, though it was one of the Formula Ford M5 cars rather than a sports racer. However, my old friend Rojer Finch and I bought two of these M5's directly from John Wyer in 1971 to use in the 1972 season. We ran the cars regularly, and they handled well, but didn't have a lot of power. We stripped an engine to discover it was unadulterated production Cortina GT, so we went to see John Wyer to complain. Sitting across from his desk, he heard our story and gave us the long glare, finally leaning back and saying: "Well, there's a valuable lesson for you for which I am not going to charge any extra!" Before we could splutter a reply he picked up his phone and arranged for a huge load of spares to be brought out to our cars. I remained good friends with the great man from then on – in fact he tried to get us some Gulf money, though that came to nothing.

The friendship was renewed on several occasions over the years, notably in 1973 when I did some endurance events in Tony Goodwin's Dulon and John Blanckley's Scorpion FVA. The Dulon shared a workshop base with the Gulf-Mirage team in 1973 at Spa, located on the old bit of the circuit between Stavelot and the new track. When Wyer was around he rarely missed the opportunity to warn me to, "Stay away from my cars!" It seems strange now that John has been gone for 20 years.

Back then, I also managed to strike up lasting friendships with Vern Schuppan and Howden Ganley, both of whom drove Mirages. It was a great pleasure to be able to share one of the 1973/74 cars with Vern at a test at Silverstone. I am indebted to them both for being so generous with their friendship and time. Vern and I shared a Ford Consul GT in the very first Avon Motor Tour of Britain in 1973, and he will regale listeners with how I shouted at him for most of the 1000 miles. He did, however, get me over being a bad passenger! Thanks are also due to Marc Devis for letting us test his car, and to Gary Pearson who was looking after it. I have been fortunate with this Veloce series to be able to test one of the subject cars for the book. That is a real privilege.

Richard Attwood was another former Mirage pilot happy to share his experiences with the author, as did John Watson, and Sir Malcolm Guthrie who bought and raced one of the early cars. Harley Cluxton also contributed and gave moral support when needed.

Thanks also to all who supplied photos: Pete Austin, Keith Booker, Peter Collins, Bob Graham, Louis Galanos, Fred Lewis, Bill Wagenblatt, Tucker Conley, Mike Jiggle, Ted Walker, Roger Dixon, Rupert Lowes, Martin Roessler, Rob Weller, Ron Forster, Peter Hoffman and others. I have done my best to credit fully, and am responsible for any errors.

I must express my gratitude to publisher Rod Grainger for his patience and understanding, as it was during the writing of this book that my wife Nancy became ill. Friends Peter Collins, Mike Jiggle and David and Lorina McLaughlin were also immensely supportive during this time, along with many others. Howden Ganley drew on his long experience of his wife Judy's illness to offer information, help, valuable contacts, his great understated humour and welcomed support.

The early years
1967 GULF M1 – 1969 GULF M2 and M3

When the FIA decreed that the World Manufacturers Championship from 1962 was to be run for Grand Touring cars, there was outcry amongst race organisers, claiming that spectators wouldn't come to races where there were no exotic machines. Subsequently, the organisers of the four main endurance races at Nürburgring, Le Mans, Sebring and the Targa Florio established the Challenge Mondiale so that prototypes could run alongside GT cars. A 3-litre limit on engine size was in place the first year, but was then dropped from 1963 through 1967. In 1966 and 1967 there were two championships within endurance racing: one for Group 6 prototypes over and under two litres, and one for cars homologated in a production run of no less than fifty cars (ie, Group 4 cars).

1967

As the 1967 season opened, not everyone realised that this would be the last year for the unlimited prototypes. The FIA had completely reversed its earlier tendency to favour GT cars, and now was promoting the prototypes. If the teams had known what was coming, 1967 would have been a less interesting year. The JW team, which would now be racing under the banner of the Gulf Oil Racing Team, knew the rule changes were coming, but considered it was still a good move to build an 'unlimited' prototype. Regulations, such as those applied to windscreen dimensions, had already changed, and Len Bailey had drawn up plans for what was essentially a GT40 which incorporated the new rules. This meant JW had a design for a car with a lower frontal area and less drag.

In the early months of the year, the team built what it regarded as a better version of the GT40. This had all the advantages of Len Bailey's aerodynamic work. The new car used a Ford engine, though not the 289 cubic inch unit.

Amongst the pile of spares that JW received from Ford after Le Mans in 1966 was a large supply of new four-bolt blocks and related components. JW assembled the blocks with a different crankshaft, and the new unit was 305 cubic inches or 4999cc. The car used the ZF gearbox, BRM mag alloy wheels, and Girling disc brakes with 11.95in ventilated discs, with larger calipers. John Horsman, in his book *Racing in the Rain*, describes the new car:

" ... a standard GT40 but the body panels were made of a very light fibreglass reinforced by strands of carbon fibre, supplied to us initially at no charge by the aircraft industry looking for alternate uses of this new material. I believe we narrowly beat McLaren as the first racing team to use carbon fibre." (Horsman, p95, 2006).

It's not entirely clear when the name Mirage was chosen for the new car. It seems that it probably wasn't too long before the first tests at Snetterton on March 21. John Wyer had asked John Horsman to put together a list of possible names, which included Falcon and Peregrine. Wyer composed his own list and when they discovered that Mirage was on both lists, the decision was made. With the Gulf backing, the Gulf colours would be used, though they opted for the lighter blue and orange combination used by Gulf in California, rather than the official darker blue. These colours would become very famous indeed over the next

Richard Attwood behind the wheel of M10001 at the 1967 Le Mans test weekend. (Courtesy Ferret Fotographics)

several years, and if there are any 'iconic' colours in racing, then they are the Gulf blue and orange.

The test at Snetterton went very well. The team's driver was to be F2 pilot Alan Rees, who had appeared in the French Matra the previous year, and was, in fact, the first driver signed up for the season. Modifications were made to springs, brakes and aerodynamics but the car ran well, though not quite as quickly as John Surtees' new Lola T70. The new Mirage was designated as an M1, with chassis number M1/10001. Wyer says in his book *The Certain Sound* that the Mirage was first designated M1/500 in light of its using the 5-litre engine, though that name didn't stick.

Though the Mirage made rapid progress, there had not been time to get it ready for Daytona and Sebring. Instead, the team ran Grady Davis' personal GT40, chassis 1049. This had been race prepared for the American Dr Dick Thompson who had raced it in 1966.

Thompson was joined by Jacky Ickx and they finished a strong sixth. Ickx was unavailable for Sebring, so another American, Ed Lowther, joined Thompson, but they retired at half distance with a head gasket failure, a problem that was to plague the team for some time.

On April 8/9, the Le Mans test weekend took place, and British driver Richard Attwood was invited to drive the Mirage.

Jacky Ickx

The son of a Belgian journalist, Ickx became a significant Ferrari sports car and F1 driver, having impressed everyone driving an F2 car in the mixed F1/F2 races in 1967, which, incidentally, also brought him to the attention of John Wyer. He was an active motorcycle racer before turning to cars, eventually driving in almost every form of competition. He became a master at Le Mans, won the CanAm title, and drove sports cars for all the major teams. He was a good development driver for Ferrari, and contributed to the Scuderia's success, though the F1 title eluded him. He remains active and holds a number of administrative posts in motor racing.

Alan Rees

Alan Rees was born in Langstone, Monmouthshire in 1938. His family was reasonably well off, and he was able to buy a Lotus 11 and then a Formula Junior, winning the British title in 1961 and driving for Lotus in 1962 and 1963. He was a driver/manager for the Winkelmann team in 1964 and had a key role in the running of that team. His Brabham took a great win in F2 at Reims that year from Clark, Brabham, Hulme and Spence. He was Rindt's F2 team-mate in 1965, and drove in F2 through 1968.

After a short spell at Matra in 1966, he joined Max Mosley, Robin Herd and Graham Coaker in founding March Engineering, all lending their initials to the company name. He worked at Shadow for some time until 1976, when he walked out with Jackie Oliver to set up the Arrows team, which he managed until 1991.

David Piper

English driver David Piper was racing seriously in the early 1950s, and has had an almost continuous history of competition until the present time. He successfully raced Lotus sports cars internationally, and by 1958 was a full-time professional driver. He went to the Tasman series in 1960, finishing second to Jack Brabham in the Wigram Trophy. He raced a Ferrari 250 GTO from 1962, and won the Kyalami Nine Hours on five occasions. He was an occasional Ferrari works driver, did Le Mans several times, and was a respected endurance driver in Ferraris and Lolas.

Dr Dick Thompson

Thompson was known as the 'flying dentist' and probably did more for the reputation of racing Corvettes than any other driver. He raced from the early 1950s until the 1970s, driving for Briggs Cunningham and John Fitch. He won many SCCA championships in the USA, and won a major race at Watkins Glen in 1963 in a Corvette Gran Sport. He never gave up his dental practice, and remained active in occasional races for many years.

41 cars were entered. Fastest times were set by Bandini and Parkes in Ferrari 330P4s, with Surtees in the Lola-Aston Martin next. The Ford MkIV of McLaren and Donahue followed, then the Ford MkII, also driven by McLaren and Donahue. Attwood's Mirage, chassis M10001, set sixth fastest time, just two seconds slower than the Ford MkII.

Attwood had driven for John Wyer, and though he was committed to a Ferrari run by Maranello Concessionaires, he was able to drive at the test weekend:

"It was very much like driving a GT40 ... a glorified GT40 with a lowered screen and the five point something engine

... I think it was a Gurney-Weslake or similar, and it was a bit faster. It wasn't a GT40 anymore, in that it was built to different rules, so it was a Mirage. It had more power, and they had taken a certain amount of weight out of it."

25 April Monza 1000 Kilometers

A second car had been completed in the three weeks between the Le Mans weekend and the team's first big event with the Mirage. M10001 was sent to Italy for Jacky Ickx and Alan Rees, and the new M10002 was to be driven by Thompson and David Piper. Ickx had a big moment in practice when his car broke a spring mounting on the banking at Monza.

In his book *Time and Two Seats,* Janos Wimpffen makes a point of praising JW team manager David Yorke for carefully putting the team's quickest and slowest drivers together. John Horsman, on the other hand, had some 'issues' with Yorke. He was critical that Yorke regularly kept Ickx in the car most of the time and Rees got very little practice – no wonder he was slowest. This eventually contributed to Rees leaving the team. The Ickx/Rees car qualified fifth, with the other Mirage sixth, a second and a half slower.

The Ickx car was an early retirement when, after only thirteen laps, the ignition amplifier burned out. The welding of the replacement brackets had damaged the electrics after practice, something which many people did not yet know about. The other car had a front damper mounting break, again due to the banking, but that, and a loose exhaust, were repaired and the car finished ninth.

May 5 – Spa 1000 Kilometers

Practice for Spa started only four days after Monza, so very little time was available for repairs. The two Monza cars went directly to Spa, while Horsman returned to Slough to oversee the final preparation of the third car, M10003, which would be sent out for Ickx and Rees. Piper and Thompson would be together in M10001, being prepared at Spa by mechanic Ermanno Cuoghi, who had been working for Ford before being taken on by JW. A very able mechanic, Cuoghi

would become one of the most well-known race mechanics of the period. A new electronic ignition system was fitted to M10001. The cars had some aerodynamic improvements after Monza – larger water radiators and rearranged twin oil radiators. Just after Monza, two new engines had arrived at Slough, two 351 cubic inch units sent over by Don Coleman at Ford. These engines had been built by Holman and Moody for Ford. One was hurriedly put into the new car, M10003. Horsman had been supervising a solution to the head gasket problem, replacing the Ford Flexitallic system with Cooper rings, which involved grooves being machined into the face of the block. There had not been time to carry out this procedure with the new, larger engine. The Cooper rings were in the smaller engine in M10001 but didn't get a very long test in the race.

In practice, Ickx again spent most time in the new car, without Rees getting many miles in at all. The new car was second on the grid, three and a half seconds behind the Mike Spence/Phil Hill Chaparral 2F. Before the race started, the tension between Yorke and Rees blew up. Rees walked out, and that was the end of his time with the team.

Ickx went out into the lead on a wet Spa track, while David Piper in the second car soon ended up in a field when a shock absorber broke. Thompson had gone to the Clubhouse when his car had retired, and the team had to track him down to get him to relieve Ickx. The team was threatened with a penalty as Ickx had driven over the maximum three hour limit, but they won by over a lap and were not penalised. It had been a fraught event, but was an impressive victory for the Mirage M1. Ford then tried to claim manufacturer's points for the win but was not allowed to do so as the word 'Ford' did not appear on the entry form.

May 28 – Nürburgring 1000 Kilometers

Four weeks after Spa, two cars – M10001 for Ickx and Richard Attwood, and M10002 for Thompson/Piper – appeared at the daunting Nürburgring circuit. Attwood was allowed to drive for JW as Maranello Concessionaires hadn't entered a Ferrari at the Ring. Both cars now had the

M10003, which Jacky Ickx and Dick Thompson took to victory after Alan Rees had left the team.
(Courtesy Paul Kooyman)

larger 351 cubic inch engines and a softer rear anti-rollbar. Then Don Coleman sent over two more 5-litre engines with Gurney-Weslake heads and one of these went into the Piper/Thompson car. A British-entered Ginetta G12 had gone off on one of the jumps, and when Thompson arrived at the same place in the first practice and did the same thing, he landed on top of it. M10002 was written-off. The surviving car managed to qualify in ninth.

Richard Attwood kindly shared the tale of his time with Mirage with the author:

M10001 at Spa, also driven by Thompson and David Piper into 7th. (Courtesy Paul Kooyman)

15

"I was driving for Maranello Concessionaires in 1967 but he (Col Ronnie Hoare) wasn't sending a car to the Nürburgring so that left me free to drive. I was selected to drive with Jacky Ickx (as a replacement for Alan Rees) and Ronnie Hoare was happy for me to drive in the Wyer team, so I did. Of course Ickx was the blue-eyed boy in the team and he was the guy who did all the running and all the setting up. Right towards the end of practice I was given a few laps because they didn't really need me. Ickx was going to do the bulk of the driving and I would only come in if they needed me, but I was clearly the 'co-driver'.

"The Porsches were quicker so they were going to have a tough problem on their hands and I realised this. So in practice, after about four laps, I was given the in board, and I ignored it because I thought that if I had to do a job here, I needed to know I was somewhere near the pace, and I did an extra lap.

"I came in after that lap, and I had gotten down to a time which I was happy with. Funnily enough, I rang John Horsman about a year ago to verify this story so I know it is accurate. I got out of the car and a little while later John Wyer said, 'Did you see that in board?' I started to reply that, 'Yes I had, but I ... .' and he stopped me and said, 'No, that's alright.' I thought I was going to get the biggest bollocking but I knew John Wyer very well and he knew me very well, and he probably knew why I was doing another lap. If however I had gone off and destroyed the car he would have been hugely not happy!

"So we did the race, and we would have won it. We were behind the one Porsche at the time, or maybe there were two Porsches in front of us as John Horsman tells me, but they didn't finish and we would have inherited the win. I think it was my last lap ... Ickx did the first stint, I was doing the middle one, and Ickx would have done the final stint ... I'm sure it was my in-lap, I was going down towards Adenau Bridge. There were some stones on the road and I couldn't avoid them all, and the back touched a big one. I could hear the hiss of the tyre and I knew that it had punctured, so I pulled over on the side by Adenau Bridge and got way over so I was out of everyone's way. I got out,

and we had a spare wheel and a jack. I started to change the front wheel, I was loosening it, and a marshal tapped me on the shoulder and he pointed to the back wheel which had also gone flat. I slung everything into the car, got in, and drove it fifty yards and burned the clutch out and that was the end of the race.

"I later rang John Horsman and asked him if he had the qualifying times, which he said he didn't have, but he did keep the race times. I was less than a second away from Ickx so at least I knew that I was on the pace, and I had never raced that car before. It was very much like driving the GT40, in fact it was a glorified GT40. They had lowered the screen a bit, and it had the bigger engine, it had some more power and they had taken a bit of weight out of it. So it felt like an over-powered GT40, and it wasn't really suited to the Nürburgring. The Porsches were much lighter and nimbler and we had to struggle to keep it on the road."

Attwood had driven the same Mirage chassis at the Le Mans test weekend, though with the less powerful engine.

It was the Porsche 910 driven by Schutz and Buzzeta which finally won at the Ring.

June 10/11 – Le Mans 24 Hours

The intention for Le Mans was to race the two surviving cars, M10001 and M10003, with the larger engines which had been rebuilt at Slough, and drive steadily in the hope of a good result. Piper and Thompson were in the former and Ickx and Brian Muir in the latter. One of the engines holed a piston, and Wyer decided to put the 305 units back in, though they did not have the Cooper ring and gasket system. Ickx and Muir were 15th in qualifying, and the other car 16th, less than a second slower. In the race, the Mirages never had a chance, as M10003 retired after only 29 laps with head gasket failure, and the Piper/Thompson car had a valve break at 59 laps, though Horsman later

Dick Thompson shared M10001 with David Piper at Le Mans, but did not finish. (Courtesy M Holocek)

Australian Brian Muir was in M10003 with Jacky Ickx at Le Mans, but also failed to reach the finish. (Courtesy Fast-Autos)

said that it also would have had head gasket failure. It was discovered afterwards that the carburettor jetting was incorrect and the fuel mixture was too lean.

July 10 – Brands Hatch 6 Hours

This race was called the BOAC 500, although in fact, it was a six-hour race. The original agreement with Gulf had included four races, all since completed. However, Gulf was quite happy to receive more exposure in the UK, so extra events were added to the schedule.

It was thus decided to send one car to Brands Hatch. As Ickx was committed elsewhere, Mexican Pedro Rodriguez was invited into the team to drive M10003. Dick Thompson was again a co-driver, as he had the support of Gulf's Grady

Davis, although John Wyer clearly felt that Thompson was in over his head.

This was a crucial end of season race as Ferrari was only one point behind Porsche in the constructors' championship. This brought some interesting drivers into the event: Ferrari had Chris Amon, Jackie Stewart, Ludovico Scarfiotti, Jonathan Williams, Richard Attwood and David Piper, amongst others. Porsche had Jo Siffert, Bruce McLaren, Udo Schutz and Jochen Rindt. There was also the Chaparral for Mike Spence and Phil Hill, as well as several potent Lola T70s.

The Lolas, with Surtees/Hobbs and Hulme/Brabham, took the first two grid spots; the Chaparral was next, and then the Ferraris. Pedro got the Mirage into ninth on the

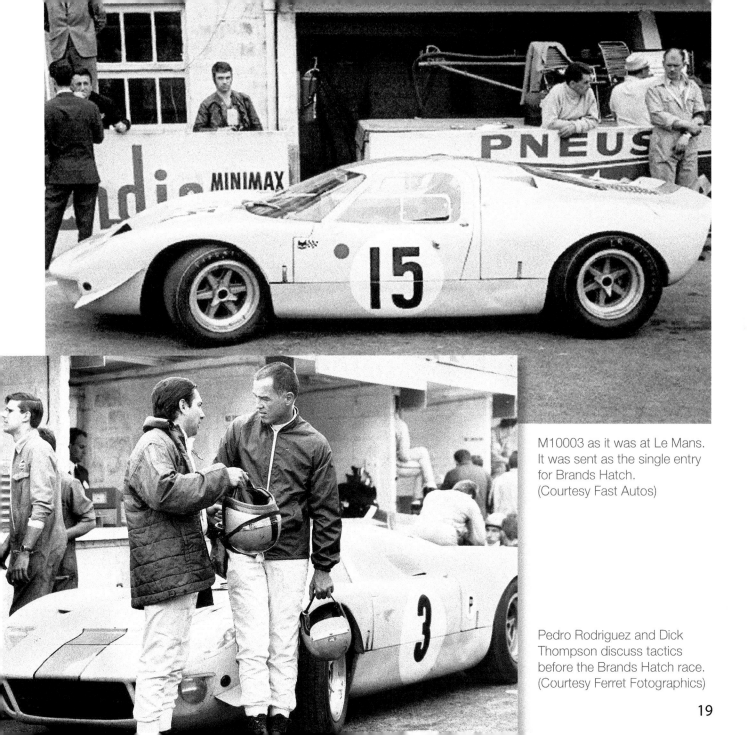

M10003 as it was at Le Mans. It was sent as the single entry for Brands Hatch. (Courtesy Fast Autos)

Pedro Rodriguez and Dick Thompson discuss tactics before the Brands Hatch race. (Courtesy Ferret Fotographics)

grid, and it looked like being a very interesting race. Although there had seemingly been some reservations about Pedro's ability as a sports car driver when JW took him on, he rather changed this view in the race. He was up to fifth in the first hour, and then third, and when the two leading cars went in for fuel, the Mirage was in the lead. The JW-Gulf stop wasn't very quick, and Thompson went out in third behind the Chaparral in the lead. Thompson lost three to four seconds a lap, and Pedro was pacing around wanting to get back in the car. After only 20 laps Thompson clouted the bank and the car was out. Phil Hill retired from racing after the Chaparral won, and, fortunately, so did Dick Thompson.

Mechanic Ermanno Cuoghi had known Pedro for some time, in the sense that they were at the same races, particularly when Pedro was in a Ferrari. Cuoghi idolized Pedro, so he revelled in their first time working together. The Mexican had asked if the steering wheel could be exchanged for a smaller one as he felt he was driving a lorry. The larger wheel had been in the package in anticipation of heavy steering which the car did not have. Cuoghi said Pedro really liked the car because you could put it anywhere you wanted on the road and it behaved itself, and that it was very neutral. Cuoghi was one of the few people who felt that Pedro had much more mechanical knowledge and set-up ability then he was ever credited with.

Pedro Rodriguez impressed with his driving of M10003. (Courtesy Keith Booker)

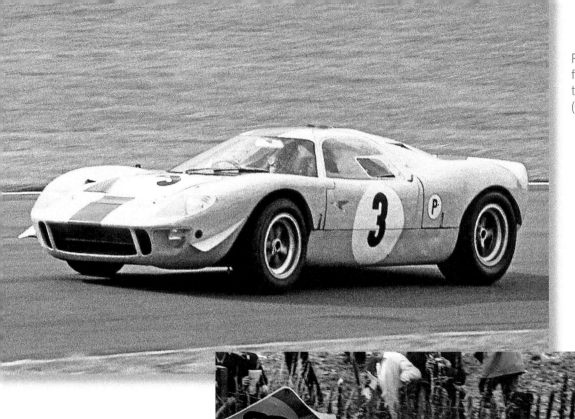

Rodriguez moved up the field until handing over the car to his team-mate. (Courtesy Roger Dixon)

Dick Thompson ended the team's fine effort by hitting the bank. (Courtesy Ferret Fotographics)

August 13 – Karlskoga

Gulf Sweden managed to persuade Grady Davis to talk John Wyer into sending two cars to races in Sweden after Brands Hatch, one at Karlskoga and the other at Skarpnäcks. Though John Horsman dismissed these as 'club races' the Group 4/6 race at Karlskoga was, in fact, a support event for the Swedish F2 Grand Prix, so there was a big crowd.

The opposition in the sports car race was indeed pretty local. M10001 was assigned to the Swede Jo Bonnier, while M10003 was in the hands of Jacky Ickx. Both cars had 5.7 Holman & Moody engines, though some of the Lolas had

5.5 litres. Yngve Rosquist's T70 was quite quick, while several GT40s looked likely to be competitive, especially that of Paul Hawkins. Ickx was fastest in practice, from the Lola and then Bonnier. Ickx eased away without difficulty at the start of the 20-lap race, but Bonnier was pushed all the way by Rosquist's Lola. Ickx won by 21 seconds from his team-mate with the Lola third, and Gunnarsson's McLaren-Elva fourth.

Skarpnäck – September 24

Ermanno Cuoghi gives an interesting account of the Swedish venture, reporting that Wyer, Yorke and three other mechanics took the long boat ride out from Hull for the first race. The cars were then taken to the Gulf refinery in Copenhagen, where they were left as the team returned to England. The next race was some six weeks away, so when they came back for the 20-lapper at Skarpnäck, all they had to do was clean the cars and set off for the circuit which was not far away.

Bonnier, again in M10001, won this race, while Paul Hawkins, replacing Ickx in M10003, followed the Swede home. Cuoghi reported that it was quite an easy win and indeed a relaxed weekend. He admired Hawkins who he considered one of the hardest-working racing drivers he had met.

John Wyer, like his mechanic Cuoghi, very much enjoyed the Swedish hospitality, though he reckoned it was "not good for the health." (Wyer, 1981, p183) The Swedish victories pleased Gulf, but Wyer was somewhat frustrated at this point. A big win had come at Spa, but he had expected to win at the Ring and at Brands Hatch, and to have much more to show for all the effort that had been expended.

He knew the rules would change at the end of the year, and that the 5.7-litre engine, and, therefore, the Mirage would not be used in 1968. With this in mind, and the fact that Grady Davis still had some money in the Gulf budget, it was decided to enter the upcoming races at Montlhéry in France and in South Africa.

Before the French race, Wyer had to fly to California with Davis to sort out a problem concerning the Mirage name. American Jack Nethercutt had built a CanAm car which he called *The Mirage*. It failed to finish in its only race, but he was arguing that he had prior claim on the name. The Gulf lawyers agreed he might be able to stop Gulf from using the Mirage name in the USA, so he was duly paid $7500 to give up his claim. Where is that car now?

October 15 – 1000 Kilometers of Paris, Montlhéry

Wyer's team decided to send only one car to the French race. While Ickx was considered the regular driver, there wasn't a consistent number two, but Paul Hawkins seemed a wise choice after his strong performance in Sweden, and he had been winning races in his own car.

This was not a championship round, though the entry was impressive, with the 7-litre Ford France car in the hands of Schlesser and Ligier which had run well at Reims. There was a Lola T70 with David Hobbs as one of the drivers, and Ferrari P3/4s for Piper/Siffert and Beurlys/Bianchi. Much effort had been put into the now Ford-powered 4.7 Matra for Beltoise and Pescarolo. This car had an amazing turn of speed, and many people thought that Matra was about to start winning races. Jaussaud and Servoz-Gavin were in a second Matra, this the 2-litre BRM motivated machine.

A number of chicanes had sprouted at the lovely circuit, including one right in the middle of the banking. This meant there would be at least four first gear corners, with a lot of strain on gearboxes and brakes. Piper and Siffert were

flying on the first day of practice and set quickest time. The JW-Gulf team was then very happy when Ickx and Hawkins improved the time on day two and took pole position. Hobb's Lola then moved up to second, with the two Ferraris on the next row, followed by the Beltoise/Pescarolo Matra. The 7-litre Ford France car was struggling with the chicane and was sixth. There was trouble for the Mirage at the end of practice. The fuel tank had been filled from the pump in the pits, which was found to contain water and rubbish, so it needed a big clean up job.

Race day was bitterly cold and grey, and rain looked imminent. The organisers, incredibly, had inserted yet another chicane in front of the main grandstand to slow the cars, and this was bound to make life even more difficult for the drivers. It was Ickx who went off in the lead. This came as a surprise to John Wyer who had flown in with his supplies man, Arnold Stafford, on Sunday morning. They and John Horsman were to do lap charts, but the signalling pits were behind the banking, a long-distance from the main pits. David Yorke shouted on the phone that it seemed that the race had started! When the rain came, it ensured a very unpleasant day for this hardy band.

After three laps, Ickx had an eight-second gap on Hobbs, Siffert, Lucien Bianchi, Beltoise, and Schlesser as Nino Vaccarella's GT40 came into the pits. Jo Siffert got his Ferrari into second, and then started closing the gap to the Mirage. By lap ten, he had gotten past Ickx. Hobbs retired on lap 15, and after one hour they had done 20 laps, with Piper/Siffert leading Ickx/Hawkins, with the Schlesser/Ligier Ford MkII in third. A number of cars were suffering from the punishment doled out by the circuit, with breakages and many spins at the chicanes. Shortly before two hours Siffert, with a 40 second lead, came in for a long stop and to hand over to Piper. The Ferrari was using a great deal of oil and dropped to sixth. Then the rain came down in torrents, and Ickx was in front and in his element. Hawkins took over but had Bianchi in the second Ferrari on his tail, with the big Ford closing.

Paul Hawkins, while not quite as quick as Ickx, did a fine job, and, by 80 of the 129 laps, the Mirage was still in front, with the Ford MkII second. As it got darker, the yellow Belgian Ferrari was flying, with Bianchi cutting the distance to Ickx, though there was a lap between them. The big Ford was struggling with handling problems. Ickx brought the Mirage home to a very impressive win in dire conditions, with the Ferrari second, followed by the Porsche 910 of Schutz and Herrmann, the Ford MkII in fourth, and Piper/Siffert fifth. A very happy JW team packed up to go home.

November 4 – Rand Nine Hours, Kyalami

John Wyer later reflected that, after the monsoon conditions at Montlhéry, the trip to South Africa was "... an agreeable way to go motor racing." It was the team's first visit to Kyalami, and the small entourage included Wyer, his wife Tottie, David Yorke, and the mechanics. Horsman was back at base attempting to sort out what JW would be doing in 1968 under the new rules. Very little had been done to M10001 which had been sent out for Ickx and his new co-driver Brian Redman. The main development during the season was curing the carburetion problems which had afflicted the 5.7-litre engine after Le Mans. A bit more weight had been removed, but the focus was on preparation, and the cars were amazingly reliable. Wyer was uncharacteristically relaxed before the race, sitting by the pool at Kyalami Ranch from where he could watch unofficial practice through his binoculars! He was quite certain that his philosophy of taking it easy and pacing in the early stages would again pay off.

David Piper and co-driver Richard Attwood had a strong history at Kyalami, having won several times, and the Ferrari P3/4 indeed was quick enough for pole position. There were two five-hour official practice sessions, several days apart. The first one was in wet conditions, but the final session was dry, and saw a number of cars beat the existing F1 lap record. Piper and Attwood were fastest, though the grid was formed on the basis of an Index of Performance formula, as the Index category was as important as overall positions. After a traditional Le Mans start, local driver Doug Serrurier led away in his Lola T70, with Dave Charlton in Sid Taylor's open T70, Mike d'Udy in a Lola and then the T70-Chev of Paul Hawkins. Hawkins had been cleaning up the African series in recent weeks and was on fine form, though last-minute work had to be carried out on the car before the start.

Jacky Ickx, as became his trademark, took his time at the beginning of the race, and held a steady position for the early laps. Frank Gardner rushed into the pits in his Lola, as the bonnet had been damaged in a collision at the start with Piper's Ferrari. Then Ickx came in on lap eleven saying the Mirage was losing oil. He was sent out again as the team realised they had over-filled the sump. After an hour and a half, Attwood took over from Piper, as Hawkins was in the lead. Attwood was then involved in a pit-lane crash with an Alfa Romeo saloon which caused a long stop for repairs and effectively put the Ferrari out of the running. Hawkins' Lola was reaching 162mph on the straight, with Piper's Ferrari at 156mph and the Mirage at 154mph. After three hours, the Mirage had eased into the lead on distance and eventually also took first in the Index of Performance. Brian Redman was an able co-driver, and the pair never lost the lead again except for a few laps when making their fuel and driver change stops. As others fell by the wayside, the Mirage pulled out an amazing thirteen-lap lead by the end, with the Hawkins/Love Lola second and Mike Hailwood and Ed Nelson third in a GT40. Piper/Attwood managed fifth. The Mirage won the Index of performance from the

---

Brian Redman

Brian was born in Burnley, Lancashire, and started racing in 1959 with a Morris Minor Estate car! He quickly advanced through a number of formulae, and drove BRMs, Shadow, McLarens and Coopers in F1. He was never entirely happy in F1, in spite of some good performances, and concentrated on sports cars and CanAm. He drove for JW-Gulf and Porsche, and became one of the most respected of sports car and endurance drivers. He continues to race in historic events, and is active in race organisation.

Porsche Carrera 6 of Tony Dean and Basil van Rooyen which was fourth on distance.

At the dinner at the end of the day, Brian Redman, whose first major victory this had been, felt the celebrations were not enthusiastic enough. John Wyer reported that Redman, with a bit of wine in him, proceeded to regale the guests with tales of the hotel trade where he had once been apprenticed, then lead a tour of the kitchens at Kyalami Ranch, and finished by singing *On Ilkley Moor ba t'at* to the assembled crowd. It was a fine way to end the season, and very few people knew that they would not be seeing a JW-Gulf Mirage again for a little while.

1968

The FIA had decided to ban unlimited engine size prototypes from the beginning of 1968, and the Manufacturers' Championship would now be run for Group 4 cars of up to five litres, of which a minimum of 50 had to be built, and for Group 6 cars of up to three litres. During 1967, the Wyer team had realised it would eventually need a 3-litre engine for the proposed Group 6 car, and that it would

M1 SPECIFICATIONS	
Presented	April 1967
Type	Two-seater coupé
Engine	Holman & Moody Ford V8
Capacity	4.9 litres/ 305 cubic inches, then 5.7 litres/ 351 cubic inches
Power	440bhp
Brakes	Girling 11.95in ventilated discs front and rear
Transmission	ZF 5Ds25/1 5-speed
Chassis	Semi-monocoque with lightweight fibreglass body
Wheels and tyres	Rubery Owen Mag 8½in x 11in, Firestone R125 or Indy 15in

never be in a position to build 50 cars for the 1968 rules. However, the team was well-positioned for 1968. Though the GT40s were getting on, it was decided to run them in Group 4 for the season. Mirage M10003 was converted back to a GT40 centre section and body shape, and renumbered GT40P/1074. Although it lost its identity as a Mirage, it seems historically important to mention briefly what it did in the 1968 season. A completely new chassis, GT40P/1075, was also built. However, according to John Horsman, this was not an ex-Mirage chassis, but an original spec GT40 chassis with some modifications. In recent years the identity of the 1967 cars has often been confused. Ronnie Spain contends that 10002 was rebuilt as 1074 and 10003 as 1075, disputed by Horsman's account. (Spain, 2003)

1074 retired at Daytona and Sebring, but, in the hands of Jacky Ickx, it was the quickest car at the Le Mans test weekend in April. That same weekend 1075 managed to win at Brands Hatch, where the new Len Bailey-designed Ford F3L appeared with the Cosworth DFV engine. Wyer had unsuccessfully tried to convince Ford to let his firm build the Ford Group 6 contender. Failing to get Bailey and the DFV, JW tried both Eric Broadley and Derek Bennett, who wanted any car they designed to be called a Lola or a Chevron, so in the end Wyer, planning for the future, opted for Len Terry to create the eventual Mirage M2. The team considered both the Eagle Weslake and Repco engines, but finally opted for the BRM V12 – probably a mistake, according to John Horsman.

Meanwhile, chassis 1074 managed to win at Monza and was sixth at the Nürburgring. 1075 took victory both at Spa and at Watkins Glen, where 1074 was second.

Le Mans had been postponed from June until September, and this provided more development time for the new Mirage project envisaged for use in 1969. The new chassis was of all aluminium sheet-metal construction with no steel bulkheads. The engine was a non-stressed member. The car had conventional suspension with unequal length front wishbones, and the rear had double radius arms on each side.

At Le Mans, Pedro Rodriguez and Lucien Bianchi managed a great victory in 1075, meanwhile 1074 (the former Mirage) had been assigned to Hawkins and David Hobbs, and that retired well into the race.

Len Terry's work on the Mirage M2 progressed through the middle of 1968, and it was finally ready for testing in August, with David Hobbs behind the wheel at Silverstone. The car suffered from overheating immediately, so Horsman carried out airflow tests. He discovered that the air just wasn't going into the side radiators. Some changes were made and the new car was taken to Snetterton the following week, this time with Robin Widdows driving. He was being considered for the 1969 line-up, but the test was short as rain made the car snap around under braking, and Widdows clouted a bank, the resulting back injury putting him in hospital with a crushed vertebrae.

November 9 – Rand Daily Mail Nine Hours, Kyalami

The sole surviving Mirage, M10001, was taken out of mothballs so that JW-Gulf could make another appearance in South Africa, after winning the previous year.

This was not a championship event and the rules allowed the unlimited engine size cars to run. Horsman had the 5.7-litre engine converted to Gurney-Weslake head configuration, with the now proven Cooper sealing rings. The main carburettor and air jet sizes were increased, the Le Mans wheels were put into use and the oil system was considerably modified.

As it turned out, the older Mirage, for Ickx and David Hobbs, was the only car over five litres, and much of the opposition was familiar, with David Piper and Richard Attwood again sharing the Ferrari P3/4. Paul Hawkins was now in an open CanAm Ferrari with John Love. Another interesting Ford was the ex-Ed Nelson car, now owned and driven by Malcolm Guthrie and Mike Hailwood, who had driven it to third last year. It now had Weslake heads and fuel-injection.

Testing went on all week, though to qualify cars only had to do three laps in daylight and three in the dark. The grid was again laid out as per Index of Performance, which put the Mirage at the front. Hawkins and Love had been quickest in practice, ahead of Piper/Attwood and then Ickx/Hobbs. Fritelli, who had crashed into Attwood in 1967, was again at the back of the grid in an Alfa Romeo.

As Ickx had not fully recovered from his broken leg at the Canadian Grand Prix, it was left to Hobbs to do the Le Mans start. But it was Belgian Teddy Pilette, 16th in practice in the VDS Alfa Romeo T33, who shot across the road and was away first. The Mirage was soon in front but the first 90 minutes saw a lot of swapping between Hobbs, Love and Piper. Malcolm Guthrie took over from Hailwood, but in only two laps he crashed and took a wheel off the GT40. At five hours, the Hawkins/Love Ferrari had a full lap lead over Ickx. At 8pm it started to rain, and Hawkins had a long stop for new tyres, then another for oil, and the Mirage led for an hour until it came in and the Ferrari was back in front. In heavier rain, Piper and Pilette collided and were both out. The Mirage then pressed on and extended its position by eight laps. When the race finished it was 12 laps ahead of the 2-litre Ferrari Dino of Dean/van Rooyen, with Hawkins and Love third and Redman/Schenken fourth in a Chevron B8. The Mirage was only eighth on Index this year, the winner being a Volvo 122S which was 12th overall!

During the two seasons in which the Mirage M1 had raced, it had won at Spa and Montlhéry, and taken the Kyalami Nine Hours twice. It was fully intended to stay part of the JW-Gulf fleet but David Yorke suddenly came to an agreement with Malcolm Guthrie whose GT40 had been seriously damaged in the race. As the car stood ready for loading in Durban harbour, Guthrie purchased the car for the remaining African races, for a price no one now can recall.

Guthrie, now Sir Malcolm, explained to the author how he got involved with the Mirage:

"I bought it because I was contracted to do the Springbok series, and I had crashed my GT40 which didn't do the roadholding a lot of good! And the Mirage came with a lot of spares but it was never going to be a GT40 – it wasn't as quick as a GT40 for a start. But we did win a race in it thanks to good ole Mike Hailwood. I don't remember what I paid for it but probably still have the papers up in the loft, along with an old GT40 side window. There are things I remember about those races ... Liz Piper was the best pit manager and knew everything that was going on."

Guthrie's memory about the comparative speeds of the Mirage and GT40 is interesting, and may reflect the fact that the Mirage was not spectacular to watch, but indeed it did get the job done.

November 23 – Cape 3 Hours, Killarney

The arrival of the now Guthrie-owned Mirage at the twisty two-mile circuit near Cape Town was a major surprise. Guthrie was going to race it with Hailwood, but as Hobbs had stayed on in the area, he was put in the car in practice,

and Guthrie decided he should share with 'Mike the Bike.' As before at Kyalami, the Springbok regulars took part, and there was a week of unofficial practice and one hour of official practice, but the grid was again determined by Index. At the 3pm start Jackie Pretorius' Lola MkIII T70 was away first, and there was the now expected battle between the Ferraris of Paul Hawkins and Piper/Attwood. Mike d'Udy's

David Hobbs

British Driver Hobbs amassed thirty years of racing experience in virtually every category including driving for McLaren, Honda and BRM in Grand Prix events, and he also did Indy, NASCAR and many long-distance sports car races. He now keeps busy as a TV commentator.

One of the many 1968 races in Africa where Malcolm Guthrie ran M10001 with some success. (Courtesy M Guthrie)

Lola was in the scrap as well. When Pretorius went off, Piper was chasing Hawkins, and Hobbs in the Mirage was closing on d'Udy – it was indeed a good race. These four fought closely for many laps until d'Udy had a puncture. When Piper also had tyre trouble, Attwood took over behind Hawkins and Hobbs. Later, Attwood had another puncture and the race ran out the race ended with Hawkins winning three laps ahead of the Mirage, and Piper/Attwood third. Guthrie was very pleased, as David Hobbs was now leading the Springbok series. Guthrie considered Killarney a 'go-kart track' and was surprised that the Mirage and any of the big cars could go as well as they did.

December 1 – Rhodesian Grand Prix – Unlimited Sports Cars

Though not a Springbok round, there were sports car races supporting the Rhodesian Grand Prix at Bulawayo, which provided the opportunity for Malcolm Guthrie to have a good 25-lap run in his new car. Paul Hawkins won in the 4.4-litre Ferrari with Mike d'Udy's Lola T70 next. Guthrie had a fine third, ahead of the flying 2-litre Chevron B8 of Brian Redman.

December 8 – Lourenco Marques Three Hours, Mozambique

There was a lot of work for some teams, as the next Springbok race was only a week later, and first practice was scheduled for Friday at Lourenco Marques in Mozambique. Several teams didn't run until the second session on Saturday. Hawkins in the Ferrari was fastest by almost three seconds from Hailwood in the Mirage, with Redman's Chevron B8 not far behind. Though this circuit has a mile-long straight on the seafront, most of it is very tight. The start grid was formed according to practice times, so everyone blinked in surprise as Redman's Chevron, Charles Lucas' Porsche 910 and Jack Holmes' Lotus Elan flashed away in the lead.

The big cars took a few laps to move to the front, and at eleven laps Hailwood was in third behind Hawkins and d'Udy's Lola. The Lola retired after half an hour, and

Hawkins led until he had to stop to clean sand from the throttle slides. Guthrie took over from Hailwood and now had a nice 2-lap lead over Hawkins. The Hawkins Ferrari unlapped itself, and a wise Guthrie decided to put Hailwood back in with 30 minutes of the three-hour race to go. This worked, and Hailwood actually increased his lead to win from Hawkins, Redman and Lucas.

Malcolm Guthrie commented on the race:

"Lourenco Marques was a wonderful place. It had a straight and that was the main road which ran along the sea. The wind blew in from the sea and took the sand onto the straight. You would barrel down the straight at 160mph, and the end of the straight was marked by straw bales on top of which sat any number of locals. Then you turned off the straight onto the circuit which was lovely. The facilities were rubbish and the loo was a corrugated iron shed with a tin can!

"And of course I was driving with Hailwood. There was a talent. Mike had a talent that he didn't realise he had. His heart was in bikes and he had done everything in bikes, and cars were just fun. If he had applied himself in cars like he had done in bikes, he could have been another Surtees. He was just a super, super bloke. He was shy, a good musician, and didn't throw his weight around."

Mike Hailwood

Mike Hailwood started racing motorcycles at age 18 and became probably the most highly-respected bike racer of all times, with many TT wins, lap records and an astonishing number of championships in all categories. His success on four wheels was not as great, though he did 50 F1 races, was on the podium at Le Mans, and was a very able sports car driver. He made a winning return to bikes in 1978. He was also awarded the George Medal for rescuing Clay Regazzoni from a fire. He was killed with his daughter in a road accident in 1981.

The Roy Hesketh circuit hosted the fifth Springbok race, and all the major runners were there, except for Brian Redman who was having some minor surgery. Piper was back with his Ferrari, but this 'go-kart track' looked to favour the smaller cars. However, it was Hawkins, Hailwood and Piper fighting it out for fastest times in practice. Mike Hailwood won one of the three bike races on his old Honda before the main event. At the start, Hawkins led, and Serrurier's Lola engine popped after five laps. Traffic was terrible as local drivers weren't watching their mirrors, and after an hour, rain made it all worse. The organisers were already in trouble with confusing lap charts. As pit stops commenced, the order changed rapidly, and through this Mike Hailwood drove superbly on dry weather tyres. Guthrie and Hailwood did a fine job of keeping the Mirage in contention, but it was now Hawkins chasing David Piper. At the very end, it appeared to everyone that Piper had got past Hawkins on the last lap, but the organisers declared Hawkins the winner from the Mirage and then Piper. No one believed this, but no protests were allowed!

The Mirage was entered at the next race at East London on January 4, but the gearbox broke and it didn't race. With the car out of the final race, Malcolm Guthrie became the pit manager for Charles Lucas who was running his Porsche 910. Lucas described him as " ... one hell of a pit manager, he really got things organised which made the race a lot easier ... he should really do it full time." Guthrie's comment was: "There must have been some crap team managers!"

1969

As the new season approached, John Wyer was very disappointed with the progress of the Mirage M2. He had originally planned for it to be ready in mid-1968 and racing by August. After the crash at Snetterton, it was rebuilt and tested again at Silverstone on December 11. The overheating had not been totally cured and they returned to Silverstone a week later with Ickx. The car suffered from low-speed understeer which turned to high-speed oversteer,

instability over bumps, and insensitive steering, and Ickx could not make it go quickly. As Wyer later admitted, at this point the team knew of possible changes ahead in 1970, so motivation for the M2 was probably lacking.

John Wyer did his utmost not to lay the blame for these problems at Len Terry's door. He was, however, clearly unhappy that Terry was not closely involved in the car's development at this stage, as had been agreed in his contract.

Wyer decided to take two GT40s, 1075 and 1076, to the Daytona 24 Hours on February 1 and 2, and to bring the Mirage M2 for a test, with a view to racing it if all was well. David Hobbs did seven hours in the Mirage the week before the race, and though there were a few minor problems, the BRM engine ran well. The difficulty was that it was not quick – even slower than Hobbs' time the previous year in a GT40. Wyer thought he had misjudged the gearing and the Firestone tyres were too small. The car only managed a top speed of 175mph – 20mph slower than the GT40 – so the car was put away. The race was won by two Lolas.

The Mirage didn't go to Sebring, but Wyer did, and two important things happened there. Firstly, the new Ferrari 3-litre prototype appeared and put some writing on the wall, and secondly Porsche asked Wyer to run the new 917s the following year. By the time he got back to Britain, the Mirage was almost a thing of the past. Wyer said it was " ... an ugly duckling which held no promise of turning into a swan!" (Wyer, 1981, p208)

April 13 – Brands Hatch 6 Hours

Nevertheless, work carried on. In March, wind tunnel tests revealed a drag coefficient of 0.395, worse than the GT40 and that was with a reduced frontal area. The team entered the Mirage M2 300/002 for Jacky Ickx and Jackie Oliver, as well as GT40 1074 for Hobbs and Hailwood.

There was a magnificent entry for this race, at which the author was present. There was a pack of Porsche 908/2s, eight Lola T70s, the Ferrari of Amon/Rodriguez, and the Ford P38 F3L which was driving Alan Mann to despair. Ickx and Oliver qualified in 11th and moved up to a competitive

Jacky Ickx talks with mechanic Ermanno Cuoghi at Brands Hatch. (Courtesy Pete Austin)

Ickx had the M2 as high as 7th at Brands Hatch before retiring. (Author collection)

looking seventh. After two and a half hours the M2 retired, Wyer saying a front suspension component broke, while others said the driveshaft had gone, and Horsman specified that it was the left-hand in-board stub yoke on the driveshaft! The GT40 finished fifth and was in fact considerably slower than the Mirage. Porsche 908s took the first three places.

Ickx crests the rise at Brands Hatch, before the stub yoke on the driveshaft broke. (Author collection)

The M2 was an impressive-looking design, though it struggled for success. (Author collection)

A serious meeting of the JWA 'clan' at Spa. From left – John Horsman, Grady Davis and John Wyer. (Courtesy Ferret Fotographics)

May 11 – Spa 1000 Kilometers

The decision had been made to miss both the Monza race and the Targa Florio, as it was clear that the Mirage-BRM would be neither ready nor competitive. The second car had been under construction during April, and Wyer was seriously hoping it would be ready for Spa. This car would not use the engine as a stressed member as with the BRM-powered machine, so the rear half of the new car was completely different. It would use a Hewland DG300 rather than the ZF gearbox. A lot of work had been done to find a way round the power loss with the BRM, due to the long exhaust pipes. Short F1 pipes feeding into a chimney in the body were tried.

When JW got to Spa, the two cars which emerged from the transporter both had BRM engines, M2/300/002 for Ickx and Oliver, and 003 for Hobbs and Hailwood. Spa saw the race debut of the fearsome Porsche 917, which could not better Ickx's 1968 time. Nevertheless the 917 was quickest until the car was withdrawn, and Paul Hawkins had his Lola T70 on pole. Ickx was next to him, making the most of his knowledge of Spa. Testing at Thruxton meant both cars had changed springs and roll bars, and GT40 driveshafts. The cars were heavy at 1650 pounds, and rather wide with the fully enveloping bodywork.

Ickx had been fastest on the first of the three wet practice days, and more work was going on with springs and roll bars. The other car of Hobbs and Hailwood was only 14th quickest, and Ickx was quoted as saying the car

was, " ... terrifying down the Masta," making it clear where he thought the blame should lie. At the start on Sunday, in the dry, to Ickx's dismay, Hawkins took off with the Belgian right behind, and Pedro Rodriguez in the Ferrari 312P having shoved past Siffert's Porsche. It was then Siffert and Rodriguez began forcing the pace with Hawkins, while Bonnier's Lola got past Ickx. On lap ten Ickx came into the pits with serious fuel starvation problems, and lost five laps as the fuel pump was changed.

John Wyer later wrote that when Ickx came in, David Yorke instructed him to switch on the fuel pump, which was only meant for starting. John Horsman described the incident in detail:

"David Yorke was the only person to hear what Jacky was reporting as the reason for the stop, which was low fuel pressure. David, without consulting JW or myself, gave one of his off-the-cuff instructions to chief mechanic Cuoghi to change the electric fuel pump. David apparently didn't realise this pump was only used for starting the car. A mechanically driven pump took over once the engine was running. The engine died out on the circuit and that was that. Jackie Oliver never got a chance to drive." (Horsman, 2006, p164)

John Wyer was critical of Yorke at dinner after the race, and Yorke got up and left the table. Wyer regretted saying what he had said in those circumstances, but he didn't think it affected his relationship with Yorke.

At 15 laps, Siffert and Hawkins led Rodriguez, who had been pushed off by a Porsche and was driving superbly

David Hobbs, on the left, contemplates a temporary problem in M2/300/003 which finished 7th. (Courtesy Ferret Fotographics)

Jackie Oliver in practice in M2/300/002, which started on the front row but ran out of fuel. (Courtesy Ferret Fotographics)

to catch up. Hobbs in the second Mirage was in 11th spot, which had been passed by Tony Dean's 2-litre 910, and even the Alfa T33 was four places ahead. At half distance, the Rodriguez/Piper Ferrari was getting closer to the Siffert/Redman Porsche. Hobbs and Hailwood had gradually moved up to seventh behind Pilette's Alfa and that is where they finished, with Siffert winning from Rodriguez, the Elford/Ahrens Porsche 908, the similar cars of Stommelen/Herrmann, Bonnier/Muller in the Lola T70, and Pilette. Hawkins and David Prophet dropped to eighth behind the Mirage.

June 1 – Nürburgring 1000 Kilometers

For the Ring, JW had now fitted one of two Cosworth DFVs which had been given to the team by Ford's Walter Hayes. John Wyer had managed to get Alfred Owen to lend him a 48-valve version of the BRM engine, so that two cars might have a chance of being competitive in Germany. The car with the new engine was chassis M3/300/001 and this was tested briefly at Silverstone. Little was learned from the test, as the vibration from the DFV shook all the needles on the gauges off their mountings, and a new arrangement had to be devised.

Ickx and Oliver had the Ford-engined car while Hobbs and Hailwood pressed on with the BRM-powered chassis. Neither was spectacular in practice. Siffert lapped his Porsche 908/2 in a fraction over eight minutes, with the Amon/Rodriguez Ferrari just behind. Then came five Porsches and then Ickx/Oliver some 24 seconds slower, with Hobbs/Hailwood the victims of poor gear ratio choice, a full 69 seconds off pole in 20th place – where the JW cars had never been before. Though much work went into the fuel strategy for the race, and Hobbs and Hailwood were running quicker than in practice, Hailwood ran out of fuel on the circuit on lap nine. The team had been given the wrong information about how much fuel had gone into the car. Ickx stopped at almost the same time with a broken left-hand rear suspension pivot bolt. It was a black day for the team, as the Porsches ran away to win, and the mighty Frank Gardner and David Piper brought the 917 home in eighth place.

The JWA team does its usual careful preparation work in the Nürburgring paddock. (Courtesy Ferret Fotographics)

Gardner always told the story of when Piper asked him why they'd been asked to drive the 917, and Frank had replied, "because they think we're pretty stupid mate!"

That was the end of the BRM-engined cars. They were sold to Jo Siffert, though he never raced them as he was very busy in the secondhand race car business in those days.

While the JW team were desperately trying to get some performance out of their new car, the ex-works M10001 of Malcolm Guthrie had been painted in grey and maroon to run alongside his new GT40 P1009. Both were entered for

The Ickx/Oliver car at the Ring, M2/300/301. Neither car finished. (Courtesy H Gustaffsson)

Mike Hailwood ran out of fuel in M2/300/003 at the Ring; another team error. (Courtesy Martin Roessler)

the Nuremberg 200 Miles at the Norisring; the Mirage for Mike Hailwood. Ignazio Giunti put the new Alfa Romeo T33 on pole, and Hailwood was ninth, three seconds slower, with Guthrie 11th. Hailwood fell back from seventh without fourth and fifth gears, finishing Heat One in 12th, with Guthrie eighth. In Heat Two, Hailwood was involved in a shunt with von Wendt which damaged the bodywork, so he was down to 13th and credited with 12th overall, while Guthrie's engine went. Redman's Lola T70 was the overall winner.

Of course by now JW had enjoyed its fabulous second victory at Le Mans in the GT40 1075 with an historic finish – the Gulf car just ahead of the Porsche. But the race had claimed the life of John Woolf, and sadly Paul Hawkins had been killed at Oulton Park a few weeks earlier, so the rejoicing was somewhat tempered.

Autosport had reported that the BRM 48-valve engine for the M2 had not yet been delivered to JW, which is interesting as it ran at the Nürburgring, and the M2 had seemingly already been sold. It may be that the M2 had been put aside and would be sold later. It was in the entry at Nürburgring but of course never appeared. Instead the DFV car was there, carrying chassis number M3/300/001/301. Was this the same car as had appeared at Brands Hatch? Well, yes and no. John Horsman had cut the roof off M3/300/001 and turned it into an open car. The weight had been reduced, though the drag coefficient probably had not been improved. Former Aston Martin employee Brian Clayton was taken on to design a new front suspension. Even though the approaching Le Mans race was taking a lot of time during this period, some testing was done. There was a new rear spoiler and canard plates at the front, and changes were made to the suspension ball joints and the dampers. The open car with no roof and the Hewland box meant the car was lighter by 80 pounds.

Wyer and his team were once again disappointed with the practice times as Ickx and Oliver could only manage fifth, nearly three seconds slower than the Redman/Siffert Porsche 908/2. Then came Pedro Rodriguez and Johnny Servoz-Gavin in a Matra 650, the Elford/Attwood Porsche, and Rudi Lins and Joe Buzzetta in a third 908/2. Just minutes before the start, while rain tyres were being fitted, a JW mechanic noticed that a front suspension mount was pulling out of the chassis. The team somehow managed to refit the original unmodified suspension parts before the flag fell. The settings had to be guessed, as the rest of the field had gone off on its warm-up lap.

Ickx came in after twelve laps to go from intermediates to wet tyres. A long stop cost two laps. Reports put this down to the team only having one hammer, but it is more likely that an attempt was being made to sort the terrible handling. Nevertheless, Ickx and Oliver both began driving very quickly and got back up to sixth. Three Porsches led Bonnier's Lola, and the Mirage was up to fifth. Then the car started weaving, and Oliver brought it in to change front tyres and have it checked. He came back a lap later and the left front coilspring/damper was changed. Ickx took over but the oil pressure was low, and a few laps later he switched off to retire. The crankshaft had cracked and destroyed a main bearing. Porsches took the first three places.

While the new Mirage was at Watkins Glen, the 'old' car, Guthrie's M10001, was entered at the Solituderennen at the 4.2 mile Hockenheim track in Germany, with Ed Nelson getting a drive. The Alfas were again on the front row: Guthrie was seventh on the grid in his GT40, and Nelson was some ten seconds slower in the Mirage. He was just joining in the battle behind his car's owner in the race when he lost a tyre tread which ripped the bodywork,

and he lost two laps having it repaired. This was a shame as Guthrie's two mechanics, Roy Ponder and George Thornton, had spent the previous week getting both the Guthrie cars immaculate. When the Alfas weakened, the Lola of Hans Herrmann took over to win.

August 10 – Austrian Grand Prix, Österreichring

Prior to the next round in Austria, rumours had been circulating that JW might have plans to run a Porsche-powered F1 car in 1970, with Jacky Ickx as the driver. The author was at the German Grand Prix at the Nürburgring at this time, watching Ickx's incredible drive in a Brabham. It was clear that he would have a big future in F1, though not quite as the rumours had suggested.

This race was the Mirage's last chance to win a championship in 1969, though Porsche had long since tied up the title. The M3 now had revised front hubs, stronger springs, stiffer anti-rollbars all round, a strengthened chassis

Jacky Ickx in the new open car, chassis M3/300/001/301, leads the Buzzetta/Lins Porsche 908/2. (Courtesy Bob Graham)

Jackie Oliver in the striking-looking, but as yet unreliable M3. (Courtesy Tucker Conley)

and a modified fuel tank. Jacky Ickx made the best of the changes by putting the car on pole on the fast, sweeping circuit. He and Oliver were a half-second ahead of Bonnier/Muller in the Lola T70, the Matra of Rodriguez/Servoz-Gavin and Jo Siffert, and Kurt Ahrens in the mighty Porsche 917. There were no works Porsche 908s, as all the effort was going into development of the 917.

On the smooth surface at Österreichring, the Mirage handling for once looked superb. As often happened, Jackie

Oliver only had a short practice period, as David Yorke let Ickx do most of the work. Oliver went well but had a spin at a slow corner, and Kurt Ahrens in the 917 piled into him, damaging the exhaust and the rear bodywork. It was all repaired in time for the race, and at the start, Bonnier's Lola got the jump on Siffert in the 917 and Ickx. Both got past Bonnier at the back of the circuit, and for the first time, a Mirage led a championship race. Both Ickx and Siffert then pulled out a lead over Bonnier and Masten Gregory in a private 908. After some laps, Siffert went in front and Gregory passed Bonnier. For many laps there was a splendid high-speed train with the 917 towing the Mirage, never more than 50 yards behind. They began to carve through traffic. On lap 24, Ickx went past Siffert and started to pull away, setting new lap records. Then the pit stops and driver changes began, and Bonnier was second and lapped by Ickx. Oliver held onto the lead, and Pedro in the Matra was second until Ahrens went past him on lap 73.

Ickx took over the wheel after the next fuel stop and regained the lead from Rodriguez, as the 917 had also pitted. Just before 100 laps, Ickx came storming in with

the steering column loose, a victim of DFV vibration. The bracket had broken, and what had looked like a sure win was now a defeat. Siffert and Ahrens got the 917 back into first place and gave the car its first victory. The M3 team recognised that if they'd had the DFV engines earlier the season could have been very different. Few people will remember how the Mirage nearly beat the Porsche 917.

September 14 – The Imola 500
There was a final non-championship race at Imola in September, and it provided the chance to do some more sorting on the M3. Springs were softened, the rear spoiler

The Cosworth DFV engine vibration eventually caused Ickx and Oliver to lose a race they were leading. (Courtesy Ferret Fotographics)

The race at Imola was the only one the Mirage M3 managed to win. (Courtesy Quintili)

grew taller, rear suspension links were relocated, the front rollbar was stiffened, and the replacement ball joints which had been removed at Watkins Glen before the start, went back in.

A single car was entered for Ickx to drive. The Alfa T33s looked to be in fine form, and at first the Mirage was having some transistor problems. Then Ickx brought the time down dramatically until a camshaft broke, so the engine was replaced. On Saturday, Ickx had knocked a full nine seconds off the previous lap record and neither the Porsche 908s, the Alfas nor the 3-litre Abarths could get near him. Would this be what JW had been waiting for all this time?

Rain had ended for the Sunday start, and though De Adamich's Alfa got the jump, it was soon Ickx into the lead on the tricky circuit, which in those days was still part public road. Though there was a great scrap between the second through tenth place cars, Ickx was picking up 1.5 seconds per lap. By lap 50 he had refuelled without losing the lead and only one other car was on the same lap. It started to rain heavily, and he came in for wet tyres on lap 61. Some cars crashed before they got to change tyres, and Ickx had time to stop four laps later to close the air intakes as he was getting flooded out! The race was due to go 100 laps, but the organisers decided to stop it at 71 laps. Ickx had a magnificent win, three laps ahead of the competent Giunti in the Alfa T33/3. It was ironic that this victory should come in the car's last race, in a non-championship event, and in Ickx's last drive for the team. The Porsche F1 rumours about Ickx driving an F1 car for Wyer floundered when, in 1970, he signed to drive for Ferrari in F1 and sports cars. Was this, then, the end of Mirage? Many people thought so.

John Wyer remembered e Imola race well, as he had put a call through to Grady Davis of Gulf to tell him the good news. When the call came through, John slipped on the way to the phone and fractured his elbow!

At the end of September came the official announcement that JW, with Gulf Oil backing, would run two Porsche 917s in the 1970 season. The announcement stated that the cars would be based at JW's premises at Slough and the works would not be entering any cars. This would turn out to be not quite what happened. The Mirage M3 would be retained should the team decide to do any non-championship races with it. John Wyer recounted that Porsche's Ferdinand Piech had said to him in the paddock at Osterreichring " ... perhaps it's good that we shall not have to race against each other again." Wyer also quoted Churchill in summarising the Mirage: " ... it died young after a long period of senile decay." (Wyer, 1981, p213)

There was a very interesting adventure which took place at the end of 1969. John Wyer, being the sort of person he was, had a back-up plan in case the Porsche deal did not reach fruition. He had John Horsman take a 5-litre engine from one of the GT40s and put it in the M3/300 with which Ickx won at Imola. Derek Bell then tested this car at Silverstone in November. Horsman was glad the Porsche arrangement had been confirmed, as the weight of this engine disturbed the fine balance the team had achieved with the DFV. This project had been called the M5, and it was put aside after Bell spun into a bank and the car was damaged.

While the JW team was turning its attention to Porsche, and the works Mirage was put aside, Malcolm Guthrie renewed his campaign using the 1967 M10001. Having won at the Kyalami Nine Hours, the car was back to be driven by Mike Hailwood and Peter Gethin, while Guthrie himself was in his GT40, sharing with Paddy Driver. A number of the 'regular' South Africa series cars had been joined by new ones, most notably David Piper and Richard Attwood in the 4.5-litre Porsche 917. Hailwood and Gethin did well to qualify the Mirage in fifth, not far off the pace at all. The M10001 ran in the top five for five hours, until it stopped on the circuit with a duff alternator. A new battery was fitted, but a few laps later the clutch failed and it was out. Guthrie had been in an accident with another car and was also out.

The Guthrie team was entered for the Cape Town 3 Hours a fortnight later, with the same driver pairings. Guthrie was running with a rather bodged tail section and the Mirage blew two oil hoses in practice. Robin Widdows was on pole with a Ferrari P4 with the Mirage next to him, until John Love pushed a 6.2-litre Lola T70 into the lead. After 10 laps Hailwood fought his way past Love, then Love led, but soon pitted and allowed d'Udy into the fight. He passed Hailwood, who came back several laps later. It was a superb race until the Mirage's engine let go and d'Udy won. There was some consolation as Guthrie managed third.

A further two weeks went by and it was time for the Lourenco Marques 3 Hours. A new engine had arrived for the Mirage, but Hailwood and Gethin had been in a rather bizarre accident in Hailwood's Iso and had hit a cow. They were not seriously injured but were not able to race. Richard Attwood, on honeymoon, took over. Gethin came to the race but had his hat pulled down to cover his face! Gear selection problems meant that Attwood did not get much running time but was fourth on the grid, with Guthrie/Driver eighth. Attwood ran much of the race in third, and after the halfway stops, was in the lead, until the Walker/Widdows Ferrari P4 went in front as darkness fell. Attwood was absolutely exhausted, and with only a few minutes to go, came in and said he couldn't continue. He was given a cold drink and sent on his way to finish third behind d'Udy/Gardner and Walker/Widdows.

The Mirage was then entered for Hailwood and Guthrie at the Bulawayo 3 Hours. It was third fastest in practice, but another engine failure meant it did not start in the race.

It returned on December 27 for the pair, but after a number of problems, it was unclassified – although it was still running at the finish.

This car, which had done so well over three seasons, then retired from period competition and returned to Britain.

In 1972 it was owned briefly by Frank Williams and Derek Robinson before going to Anthony Hutton. Hutton entered it for the Silverstone Interseries race on May 20, 1973, but a wishbone broke in practice and it did not race. It was by this time back in Gulf colours. On August 27 it finished sixth at Brands Hatch in the *Motoring News* GT race, in Hutton's hands. It was then swapped to Paul Weldon for GT40 1034.

M10001 in the 1970s, racing at Thruxton. (Courtesy Peter Collins)

Anthony Hutton races M10001 at a Silverstone historic race in 1973. (Courtesy Peter Collins)

Weldon and Hutton each won three Paul Hawkins Trophy races with the car. It was sold to David Mulvaney in late 1974, then to Harley Cluxton in the USA, then to Jo Shoen and on to Terry Clark, who ran it in American historic events. It went to Bill Konte in 1984, and later was restored by Harley Cluxton. Sometime after 1984 it was passed to the Blackhawk Collection, which has the car for sale for the current owner at the time of writing this book (but may now have changed hands again). Don Williams of the Blackhawk Collection confirmed for the author that M10001 is indeed the only surviving Mirage M1.

M2 SPECIFICATION

Presented	August 22, 1968
Type	Two-seater closed coupé
Engine	BRM V12
Capacity	2999.5cc
Power	375bhp
Brakes	Girling 11.9in discs all round
Transmission	ZF 5-speed
Chassis	Aluminium alloy central monocoque section with tubular steel subframe
Wheels and tyres	15in diameter cast magnesium, front 9.5in rear 12.5in, Firestone tyres

M3 SPECIFICATION

Presented	May 1969
Type	Two-seater open car
Engine	Ford Cosworth DFV V8
Capacity	2995cc
Power	430bhp @ 10,000rpm
Brakes	Girling ventilated discs all round
Transmission	Hewland DG300 5-speed gearbox
Chassis	Aluminium alloy central section monocoque with tubular steel subframe
Wheels and tyres	15in diameter cast magnesium, front 9.5in rear 12.5in, Firestone tyres

Running with the best
1972/1973/1974 GULF M6 and GR7 – 1975 GR8

1970 and 1971 were hugely successful years for the JW-Gulf Team and for Porsche. Wyer's organisation won eight of the 1970 races in the 917 and 908/3, Porsche took the Manufacturers Championship with 63 points to only 37 for Ferrari, and Pedro Rodriguez and Leo Kinnunen scooped 105 points each to Jo Siffert's 100 in the drivers' standings. Porsche also won the Grand Touring Trophy, the Challenge Mondiale, the Marques' Standard Points, and the Marques' Triple Crown championships. The JW 917 provided some of the most exciting sports car racing ever seen, with Pedro's drive at Brands Hatch in the wet considered the best thing ever seen by those who were there. However, Porsche politics had raised its somewhat unpleasant head, and Porsche reneged on its agreement to support only JW, while works-supported Porsche Salzburg stole Le Mans from the blue and orange team.

In 1971, JW took five of the year's eleven races. Hans Dieter Dechent's Martini Porsche team took three after buying the Porsche Salzburg cars and running in a semi-works capacity, while Autodelta's Alfa Romeos won three times – at Brands Hatch, the Targa Florio and Watkins Glen. Porsche still won all the international categories, and Rodriguez again topped the drivers' table ahead of Andrea de Adamich. But both Rodriguez and Siffert were killed in 1971, the Mexican at the Norisring in a private Ferrari, and the Swiss at Brands Hatch in his works BRM. These deaths had a powerful impact on the team and on John Wyer personally.

The period 1972 to 1975 saw a major rule change as the 5-litre cars which had so dominated the previous two years were now out of date, and the 3-litre prototypes were back. Unlike the previous 3-litre cars, however, these were thinly disguised F1 cars, and though they were often as quick or quicker than the 917s and 512s, they didn't have the aura and spectacle of the bigger machines, and the public was less drawn to them. However, the manufacturer interest kept the series going, perhaps for longer than some would have predicted.

Wyer was very proud of the performance the JW Gulf team had managed, and was very disappointed at the end of 1971 when there was no acknowledgement of this at all. Then Porsche announced that Roger Penske would be running the CanAm effort in 1972, with no word to Gulf or JW about this beforehand. Wyer decided he no longer wanted a front-line role, and had turned down an earlier offer to go work with Gulf. Wyer then agreed to act as a consultant, and, as he and Grady Davis had great faith in John Horsman, they set up a small subsidiary company called Gulf Research Racing at Slough, with Davis as president and Horsman as managing director. Wyer would be a non-executive director, and would be brought back for a short spell in 1975 as president when Davis retired. Wyer later made it clear that he fully believed the return to three litres was disastrous for sports car racing, and made it very much a poor relative to Grand Prix racing.

1972

The name of the new company was released in January. *Autosport* announced that the team would run a Group 5 Mirage with a DFV engine designed by Len Bailey, and would debut at Sebring in March, possibly with Derek Bell and Gijs van Lennep as drivers. David Yorke had left the team to go to Tecno, and chief mechanic Ermanno Cuoghi wanted to return to Italy, where he was taken on by Ferrari. Alan Hearn and Ray Jones took over Cuoghi's role, with several of the other JW team of recent years also staying on.

The car first appeared at Silverstone on March 14 with Bell behind the wheel. Bailey and Wyer were present to watch the Gulf-Mirage M6, whose debut had already been delayed by non-delivery of parts blamed on the coal miners' strike. The monocoque tub was reinforced by mild steel sub-structures, skinned in 18 gauge L72 aluminium alloy except for some of the semi-stressed panels. Side pontoons carried two 60-litre fuel tanks and pumps. The car was designed so that it could use either the DFV or a Weslake V12. Thus with the V8 installed, there was room in the engine compartment for cooling, and a degree of flexibility as to where mountings and brackets could be fitted. There were fabricated steel rear suspension crossmembers. The lower rear suspension mounts were via a magnesium casting bolted under the gearbox, with front suspension by lower wishbones, fabricated top links, trailing arms and outboard coil/spring damper units. There were hub-mounted front and rear Girling ventilated disc brakes. The car ran on Goodyear tyres for 25 laps before the drive to the mechanical fuel pump (which also drove the oil pump) failed. However, a few days later at Goodwood it achieved more laps – a total of 169 miles – before being shipped off to Sebring. The car had been late arriving at Slough, so there were real worries about the limited testing.

March 25 – Sebring 12 Hours

Ferrari had already won the first two championship races, demonstrating how well its 3-litre car could perform. John Horsman was even more worried by the DFV-powered Lola T280 (with a Hewland box like the Mirage) as that had been also running very strongly.

The Mirage M6, in the hands of Bell and Dutch driver Gijs van Lennep, was clearly too new for racing, and more testing was definitely needed, though it showed promise. In the first practice sessions the car would only do a few laps before it overheated. A hose came off and Bell thought he was on fire, lost concentration and had a nose-damaging excursion. The overheating was traced to poor flow through the radiator – sorted by Horsman and his team by reversing the direction of flow. Gear ratios were borrowed from the Lola team, and the car went better, although the fuel pressure was too low to work properly. After another damaged nose,

Derek Bell joined the Mirage team in the 1972 season, having raced for JW in Porsches. He is shown here at Sebring with journalist/commentator Chris Economaki. (Courtesy Lou Galanos)

the Mirage was nine seconds slower than Andretti and Ickx's Ferrari, though still seventh fastest overall.

The three Ferraris of Andretti/Ickx, Regazzoni/Redman and Peterson/Schenken just cleared off at the start, with one of the Alfas trying to hang on. The Lola was in the pits with a broken wishbone on lap three, but the Mirage was in two laps later with Bell reporting a severe vibration; a tyre change solved that problem. The clutch then failed and it was discovered that the clutch pushrod was missing, which was replaced but it disappeared again. This precipitated a three-hour pit stop to change the clutch, flywheel and clutch release mechanism. Then the throttle stuck open with sand in it, a rubber driveshaft coupling broke, and the differential gave up. The Mirage had only managed a total of 48 laps. Horsman later found out that the experimental Vandervell coating on the inside of the tube holding the clutch throw-out bearing hadn't worked, which had resulted in the tube seizing on the input shaft. This was not discovered, unfortunately, until some time later.

Derek Bell
Bell is of course one of the most successful of all long-distance drivers. He started racing a Lotus 7 in 1964, moved up through F3, F2 and into F1, where he drove for Ferrari, Tecno, Surtees and McLaren. He won Le Mans five times and the Daytona 24 Hours three times, and was awarded an MBE for services to motorsport. He remains very active at historic events and splits his time between the UK and the USA.

Gijs van Lennep
The Dutch driver, like Bell, drove in F1 but is mostly known for his many sports car successes, especially in Porsches. He drove for Surtees, Frank Williams and the Ensign team, and won at Le Mans in 1973 with Helmut Marko, the Targa Florio that year, and took another Le Mans win in 1976 with Jacky Ickx.

Derek Bell drove the new M601 very hard at Sebring, though it still needed development work. (Courtesy Lou Galanos)

Gijs van Lennep in M601 on the Sebring airfield circuit. (Courtesy Tucker Conley)

The car receives attention in the pits. (Courtesy Tucker Conley)

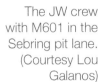

The JW crew with M601 in the Sebring pit lane. (Courtesy Lou Galanos)

Derek Bell pushed M601 into 10th place on the grid at Brands Hatch. (Courtesy Gulf)

April 16 – BOAC 1000, Brands Hatch

Almost one year since Len Bailey had been given his brief to design the Mirage for 1972, it was about to enter its second race. After Sebring, Horsman had managed to obtain some very expensive titanium springs à la Porsche 917 to replace the steel springs already on M601. This immediately improved handling. Some testing at Goodwood showed that the overheating issues had seemingly been resolved, though when M601 went to Brands Hatch for the weekend, it was still three seconds slower than the Ferraris and two slower than the Lola. The spring change had helped the handling on the demanding Kent circuit, but Bell stopped with no electrics. Some hard work was done but 10th place

on the grid was the result, and the Mirage was still three seconds from the Ferraris, all at the front.

Bell was into the pits on only the fourth lap of the race on Sunday, the car overheating once again. This cost some 24 minutes and all hope of a result. He returned to the pits for another long stop, the temperature reading right off the gauge. Some time later, Bell stopped at Dingle Dell and came back to the pits with his 'spark box' in his hand, and then set off with another to replace it, already 49 laps behind. Van Lennep had yet to race the car, so when Bell finally brought it in for fuel, van Lennep jumped in and set off. The car was lapping quite well for a period here, making up laps, but soon the Dutch driver was in with

M601 is worked on in the rather
shabby Brands Hatch paddock.
(Courtesy Rob Weller)

Van Lennep holds off the Alfa
Romeo of Revson and Stommelen.
(Courtesy Pete Austin)

a broken gear linkage and another very long stop. The car was indeed running at the finish, having done 117 laps, but that was too few for it to be classified. The three different radiators tested at Goodwood hadn't done the trick, and the car was still suffering from lack of testing. Thus it was taken to the Nürburgring immediately after the Brands race for further development. This meant missing the race at Monza, as did the Autodelta team, so Ferrari had another easy win there.

However, the Nürburgring test was reported as very productive, with Derek Bell doing over 500km with no failures. Bell managed a lap just under Ickx's 1971 time in the Ferrari, and now the overheating problems did indeed seem to have been solved. A number of other relatively minor adjustments were made and the Gulf Research Racing team left the Ring in better spirits. Apparently, the team had pointed out several times to journalists at Brands Hatch that it was Gulf Research Racing, with the emphasis on research, though few people were fooled by that. The next race would be a real test for the Mirage.

May 7 – Spa 1000 Kilometers

Autodelta was still working on the Alfa T33s so it also missed Spa, as well as Monza, where the field was not nearly as exciting as it had been the two previous years. The Grand Prix Drivers Association had tried to boycott the Spa circuit for being too dangerous, and the Grand Prix had moved away from the Ardennes. However, a compromise was reached, and the GPDA members were not banned from racing there, though Jo Bonnier decided not to drive – ironic in view of later events. The author was a GPDA member for a short time in those days when new secretary Nick Syrett decided to admit drivers from other categories to carry out various tasks and provide a wider perspective. It was something of a coincidence that the author was also racing a Mirage that weekend back in the UK. This was one of the small number of Formula Ford M5s.

Ickx and Regazzoni put the Ferrari 312P on pole on three seconds quicker than the similar car of Redman/Merzario, and a full sixteen seconds faster than the third

Ferrari of Peterson/Schenken. The Lola T280 of Larrousse/de Fierlant was almost six seconds behind Peterson.

In Thursday's practice, the Mirage was suffering from a misfire and was well off the pace. The car was using a narrower, full-width rear wing, and the springs had been changed yet again. Tyres had now been switched from Goodyear to Firestone, but only Firestone slicks were available as intermediates could not be finished on time. Some further sorting by Len Bailey saw an improvement to 3min 42.5s, but this was still not good enough. A broken lower front engine mount bolt had been replaced, and both Bell and van Lennep complained that the car felt very light at the rear, the Dutchman having a lurid spin at Les Combes at the top of the hill on the very fast 'old' circuit. The settings were then returned to those employed at the Goodwood test and, using the wider rear, wind helped the handling. The drivers then had no time to get used to the new settings, but the car felt more secure.

The Mirage was sixth on the grid behind the three Ferraris, the Lola and the Jost/Kauhsen Porsche 908/3. With light rain falling just before the start, Larrousse in the Lola was in a state as he was on slicks and the Ferraris in front of him were on a combination of wet and dry tyres, so he switched to intermediates at the last moment. The start was a shambles, with the betting being that there was a 'deal' between the starter and Ickx! There was a slight collision between Bell in the Mirage and the Lola, and the field became well strung out, John Hine having pushed the 2-litre Chevron into fourth place. Ickx led the Ferraris across the line at the end of the first lap chased by the Lola, and Bell was catching the Jost/Kauhsen Porsche 908/3. He got by on the next lap, but the Lola was hanging onto Schenken's Ferrari and then Larrousse got by on lap eight – a sign of what a DFV-engined car could do.

The Porsche retired with a fuel leak around the one hour mark. The Ferraris were having 'chunking' problems with their tyres, and then the Lola had a long stop, so Bell got the Mirage up to fourth, ahead of Hine's rapid Chevron. The Lola was sixth, now driven by de Fierlant. John Gray in the other Chevron, shared with John Lepp, crashed at

Les Combes at the two hour mark, slowing the whole field for a few laps. Van Lennep took over from Bell at the second stop, but then stopped at the top of the hill to tighten his seat belts, yet managed not to lose a place. Then van Lennep was soon back into the pits, however, with a misfire and a faulty throttle linkage. This dropped the Gulf car to sixth, though the Lola was soon in trouble when a stone broke the brake master cylinder and a long stop followed. The Mirage was now sounding healthier in fifth place.

The Ferraris made what were meant to be their final stops, Regazzoni taking over from Ickx, and Redman from Merzario. Then Regga didn't come around for some time, finally limping in with damaged bodywork where a tyre had come off the rim. Peterson had taken over from Schenken and was chasing Redman fiercely for the lead. He was closing the gap when he slid on something at Les Combes and flew into the guardrail, and Ferrari was now down to two cars. Rain started as Redman cruised to the win, while Ickx/Regazzoni held onto second. John Hine and

John Bridges had a fine third in the Chevron, which could not be caught by the Mirage, that car being hampered by a wet and misfiring engine. The Lola got back up to fifth behind Bell and van Lennep. Merzario's win with Redman meant he had lost a strange bet with Regazzoni, and Regga got to cut Merzario's long hair in the pit lane! It had been a good race with a rather small field, and was somewhat encouraging to the Gulf team which had at least finished.

May 28 – Nürburgring 1000 Kilometers

Ferrari had absolutely no intention of sending any cars to the Targa Florio two weeks after Spa but the organising body prevailed on Ferrari to relent, so they quickly put softer springs on one of the cars. Ferrari's Art Merzario and Sandro Munari did a brilliant job of winning, ahead of two Alfas who were very disappointed because they had put so much preparation into the Sicilian event.

For the Nürburgring, where the Mirage M6 had gone well in testing, a new ram air intake box borrowed from

M601 managed a reasonable 4th place at Spa. (Courtesy Landmann)

Frank Williams was fitted, along with the team's rebuilt series 12 DFV engine. A larger alternator had also been fitted, along with a rubber covering for the distributor to protect it from the wet. This was needed for the very changeable conditions of the pratice run. Bell was impressed with the extra 500 revs he was getting from the new airbox, and wished he'd had it at Spa. Very few cars achieved quick laps, since much of the five-hour Friday session was wet. Bell spent time in the pits when the steering rack was being changed, and the newly rebuilt engine was fitted in the evening in the hope of some dry laps on Saturday.

But it was wet again, and when it dried out for a short spell, it was Peterson who was ready and took advantage of the situation to record a time of 7min 56.1s for pole in the Ferrari. Van Lennep was also ready, but he was only having his first drive of the weekend and did very well to get round in 8min 8.8s for second place on the grid. That was indeed heartening for the team as the potential of the Mirage was again demonstrated. Two Alfas were next ahead of the Jost/Casoni Porsche 908/3, then the Redman/Merzario Ferrari. Hine and Bridges were quicker in their Chevron than the Ickx/Regazzoni Ferrari, though no one really expected it to stay that way in the race.

For the start it was wet but not raining, so tyre choices were difficult. Bell had a hesitant start and was in fourth behind Peterson, Stommelen's Alfa and Merzario. At the end of the lap, it was Ferrari in front as usual, and by the third tour it was Ickx, Merzario and Peterson, with Bell having left the Alfa behind. The Ferrari dominance was obvious as the red cars pulled out ten seconds per lap on the Mirage which was going very well. By lap 14, things were

changing. The Ferraris had been in for their stop and Bell had moved up. With a better choice of tyres, the Mirage was closing on the Ferraris. On lap 17 Regazzoni hit the fence at Wipperman in his ill-handling car and Bell got past – the Mirage was at last leading a major race.

Derek Bell in the pit lane at the Nürburgring in M601 which ran as high as 2nd but finished 4th. (Courtesy Gulf)

Van Lennep in the Karussell at the Nürburgring. (Courtesy Ferret Fotographics)

However, it was a short lead as Bell handed over to van Lennep. After the stop, and by half distance, van Lennep was still in second, two minutes behind Peterson, though Merzario was now catching the Mirage. During the next stop Bell took over again, but he was feeling unwell. The dampers had been altered, and a new set of slicks had been fitted. The Ferraris had stayed on intermediates but the track was now drying. The Mirage was down to third after the stop but in eight laps Bell had gotten back to second. He was feeling ill but driving well. He was given the go signal on lap 43 and was really flying, though the gear selector was now working only intermittently. Then the DFV engine gave up. The Redman/Merzario Ferrari got past into second and the Marko/de Adamich Alfa third and the Mirage was credited with fourth place. Peterson had switched to slicks just to make sure the Mirage couldn't catch him, but it certainly had threatened to do so.

The decision by Grady Davis to skip Le Mans meant the team had time to build up a second car and do some thorough preparation for the next race, which would be in Austria at the end of June. Matra conquered the 24 Hours, the only race they wanted to do in 1972. Ferrari didn't go, so Matra had a free hand. They were very worried when one of the MS670s blew an engine on the second lap, but Graham Hill and Henri Pescarolo won, with Francois Cevert and Howden Ganley taking a superb second, while the venerable 908/3 of Jost and Casoni came in third. A third Matra of Jabouille/Hobbs should have come next but was not running at the finish, so fourth place went to the de Adamich/Vaccarella Alfa 33TT3. Sadly, it was in this race that Jo Bonnier was killed when his car flew into the trees on the straight.

June 25 – Österreichring 1000 Kilometers

Before the Austrian race, *Autosport* reported that the Gulf test programme was continuing, that two cars would appear at Watkins Glen, and that work continued on the Weslake V12 (which was giving 450bhp on the test-bed). It was thought a new car with bulkheads specifically designed for the V12 should be ready for the Montlhéry race later in the year.

What Horsman and his mechanics set out to do in this 'break' period was to build M6/602 as a second, race-ready car, and prepare M6/601 as the back-up for the next event. To improve grip at the front end, the front blade was extended to two inches, and some small side fences were added to provide a degree of downforce. The cars were then taken to Austria the week before the race for private testing. Horsman had taken on board the competent American driver Tony Adamowicz to do some of the testing, as well as to provide some coverage for Gulf in the USA.

The Mirage had been running on 13in diameter wheels and the team now went for 15in on the rear, while rim widths remained at 11in/16in. The testing did not go smoothly. There were both fuel pressure and oil temperature problems. Air ducts were made to force cool air to fuel pumps, and the pressure relief valves were changed time and again before the engine was 'right'. The clutch release bearing on M6/602 failed, and then the flywheel bolts all broke. The car got down to some reasonable times, not far off the Rodriguez lap record of 1971 in the JW 917. Adamowicz was down as a third driver for the upcoming race, but it was not expected that he would race, though he was due to appear at Watkins Glen.

There was a fourth Ferrari present for Helmut Marko and Carlos Pace. Sandro Munari was with Merzario, and Regazzoni was absent. It rained, as had been the recent custom, in the first practice session. Van Lennep was out in the 'T-car', M6/601, and set some good times. On Saturday it began to look like the rain would come again so everyone was anxious to get in a good time. Bell was out and going very quickly in the new car, getting down to 1min 40.6s, with van Lennep and Adamowicz sharing the other car. Bell was on the softer compound Firestone tyres, so Ferrari decided to switch to those, but waited too long and the rain appeared. The Mirage was on pole, and the Elford/Larrousse Lola was 7/10 slower, with the Ickx/Redman Ferrari just behind. The Ferrari team showed so much interest in the Mirage that there was apparently an offer to put the Ferrari engine in the Mirage chassis. All the Ferrari drivers were impressed by the handling of the M6, though the proposal never got beyond that.

Saturday was dry for the start, and Ferrari was in a panic about understeer. However, Bell made a cautious start and four Ferraris were off into the lead, and soon the Lola was past the Mirage, though it was very quickly into the pit when Larrousse had the throttle cable jam, and lost two laps. Bell's cautious start turned out not to be intentional. A new DFV had been installed before the race and it misfired from the start. In spite of the problem, Derek Bell drove an inspired race. He caught and got past Merzario, and chased Tim Schenken lap after lap, until it was time for the routine stops. Bell went in, only to lose time while a split header tank was replaced, but that was not the only problem as the engine was again running rough. John Horsman described the incidents:

"Over the next 105 laps the spark box was changed twice, the mixture adjusted three times, the spark plugs changed three times. In addition the battery died and was changed, and the tyres shifted position on the rims, causing an out-of-balance condition, and had to be changed twice." (Horsman, 2006, p288)

The car was retired at three quarters distance and it was not until the team tested again at Goodwood the following week that a DFV cylinder head was found to be porous and that fluid had been getting into the cylinder. Cosworth replaced the cylinder head at no charge which they didn't often do, but Horsman felt that was little compensation for the disappointment in Austria where a win was a possibility. Ickx and Redman took the win ahead of the other three team cars, with a Chevron B21 getting fifth.

July 21 – Watkins Glen Six Hours

With deeper radiators and dual oil coolers, the two cars appeared at Watkins Glen in the USA almost a month later. They would need the new additions, as Watkins Glen provided the hottest temperatures of the entire season. Carlos Pace had been brought in to share M6/602 with Derek Bell, and van Lennep and Adamowicz would be in M6/601.

The Watkins Glen track had been revised so previous times didn't mean much. What was important was the heat, and the fact that circuit was very hard on brakes and tyres. Firestone engineers said they had only recorded a higher track temperature once before at Bulawayo, so Ferrari and Mirage went for the harder compound tyre. The Mirage found new speed from a sorted set of engines but then a new problem appeared – the brakes were not up to the stress, and the fluid was boiling, something which the team mechanics said they had never seen before. The Mirage was running smaller brakes and did not have enough ventilation to cope with the conditions. Jacky Ickx was timed at 182mph while the Bell/Pace Mirage was next at 180.9mph. The second car was struggling with an engine that didn't have enough revs, though the Gulf drivers were all happy with the superior handling of the cars. Peterson/Schenken led the grid from Ickx/Andretti, with the Bell Mirage third, ahead of Redman/Merzario, Larrousse/Wisell in the Lola, Adamowicz/van Lennep and Americans Scooter Patrick and Milt Minter in a private Alfa Romeo T33/3.

The two lead Ferraris blasted away at the start, neither Peterson nor Andretti prepared to give a single inch at the start of a six hour race. Bell was ragged but hanging on to the two leaders, and then Wisell in the Lola was up to fourth. As had happened before, the Lola was in trouble early, Wisell going off on the second lap and being hit by a Corvette. Patrick in the Alfa joined it after a dozen laps when he had been running ahead of the Jost Porsche 908/3. Then a few laps later Bell was in the pits to report overheating. He was sent out again just ahead of his team-mate, but three Ferraris had gone by and Derek could not get back on terms with them, though he tried very hard. The Andretti/Ickx car was also afflicted with heat and a stop saw them drop back, their chances not looking very good.

Bell was back in on lap 37, with smoke pouring from the brakes, the fluid boiling, as the seals had burst. During the repairs there was a minor fire in the engine bay, but a marshal had that under control fairly quickly, and the Bell/Pace car was now in sixth. Van Lennep came in not long after this, and said his brakes were overheating, to be followed by Pace again in a few laps with smoke pouring out of the other side, and again the seals were gone.

Adamowicz bravely took over M6/601 but soon had no brakes, and had a spin avoiding another car. He hit the guard rail with the back of the car, damaging the body section, bent the exhausts and broke off the gearbox end plate. The pit stop lost them 15 laps. The team did get it going again but now second gear kept sticking and the throttle was jamming. Back in the pits, a fuel overflow dripped onto the exhaust and Mirage had a second fire to deal with. John Horsman jumped in and sorted this one, and the car was able to continue, though it rather stuttered out of the pit lane. After 141 laps and heavy use of the gearbox to slow down the brakeless car, the box gave up and seized out on the circuit, blowing a tyre in the process.

There was still a long way to go. Ickx and Andretti now controlled the front, with Peterson and Schenken not far behind. In fact, they resumed their earlier battle and the final half hour was tremendous with the two cars finishing only fourteen seconds apart. Meanwhile, Bell and Pace cruised on steadily into third place in M6/602, but they were 14 laps adrift of the Ferraris. It wasn't much of a reward for all the effort but at least this valiant and determined pair had gotten a very wounded car to the finish.

Van Lennep and Tony Adamowicz in M601 had mixed fortunes at Watkins Glen. Here, they hold off Redman's Ferrari. (Courtesy Ron Forster)

Bell and Carlos Pace brought M602 home to a solid 3rd place. (Courtesy Ron Forster)

The staff who had remained at Slough while the race team was at Watkins Glen, had been getting on with the construction of M6/603 which would carry the Weslake V12. Though Dan Gurney had advised against its use, Horsman and Wyer wanted to press on. While it had seemed earlier in the year that the M6 chassis might take either engine, the V12 required a number of changes, including a longer wheelbase. The engine was said to be reaching 460bhp at 10,600rpm.

Derek Bell was able to test the new combination for the first time on August 12 at Goodwood. The water temperature was again high, and ducting was needed to cool the front brakes and various radiators. Different means of improving cooling were tried over the two day test. After some 216 miles, the new car was still a second and a half slower than the best time the previous April with the DFV.

A second Weslake V12 was tried a fortnight later, again for two days, and the time was cut by half a second. There was a misfire that was cured by a mixture change, and a number of other problems which Horsman felt should have been sorted on the dyno by Weslake during factory tests of the engine. Almost 500 miles was done on the M6/603 chassis and nothing had broken. In a 'quiet' period, Derek Bell went out in M6/601 with the DFV, and went two seconds faster. A third test with the V12 in the M6/603 was carried out in mid-September, but this time the misfire could not be cured. Late in September, more testing was done to compare tyres and various makes of brake pads. On October 2nd, Howden Ganley

American Tony Adamowicz enjoyed his short period as a Mirage driver. (Courtesy Ron Forster)

and Carlos Reutemann shared the testing on M6/601, attacking handling and cooling problems, and making considerable progress. The V12 tested again in October at Goodwood and though there was no misfire, the torque rating was poor.

Both cars went to Silverstone on November 14, and Bell was two seconds slower than Ganley. Bell was in the V12, and Ganley the DFV. A week later, with a changed V12, the two cars were only a tenth of a second apart, so only one of the Weslake engines actually seemed to be performing well. Gurney had said to the team that Weslake, " ... could not build two engines the same."

Of course, there was no championship race at Montlhéry so the story that the V12 would appear there

Derek Bell in for his routine stop. It would appear to be John Horsman in the distinctive hat at the back of the car.
(Courtesy Ron Forster)

never came to be. Ferrari had won the Manufacturers' Championship by a massive 208 points to Alfa Romeo's 85, with Mirage sixth on 32 points. Ickx led Schenken, Peterson, Redman and Andretti in the driver ranking.

Howden Ganley talked to the author about his venture into the Mirage team:

"Late in 1972 I received a phone call from John Horsman asking if I would come to Goodwood and do some tyre testing. I had done some work with the team before on the development of another car. It was mainly to do some testing. I was supposed to be going with Matra for 1973 but suddenly all the non-French were redundant ... no 'rosbifs' or Kiwis! John gave me the impression that this was a tyre test and nothing more. I was then invited back to so some more the following week and that was a back-to-back test of Goodyear versus Firestone, and I came to the conclusion that there was not a great deal of difference between them. Horsman then said to me: 'You seem to get on pretty well with the car ... would you like to drive for us in '73?'

"At that point it was just Derek and me, and then they were trying others who turned out to be Mike Hailwood and John Watson. We then came back again to test, and Derek and I each drove both cars to see what we each thought of one car versus the other. My impression was that the Weslake was actually quicker down at the end of Hanger Straight and then coming back up to Woodcote, but it took a while to get there, and the DFV car was much more agile and would get into and out of the corner, whereas the Weslake car was longer and heavier, and had a higher centre of gravity and was just harder to drive. The Weslake had a higher top speed and would be good at Silverstone and Le Mans. The times were good with the one good engine, but it was too risky for the team to go with the Weslake."

1973

Midway through January, *Autosport* announced that the driver line-up for 1973 would include Bell, Ganley, Hailwood and Watson. The magazine's technical editor John Bolster visited the GRR premises at Slough and had

Carlos Pace

Brazilian Pace was a contemporary of the Fittipaldi brothers. He arrived in Europe in 1970 and won the Forward Trust F3 Championship. F2 in 1971 was not successful, but he nevertheless drove an F1 March for Frank Williams. He was in the 1973/74 Surtees F1 team, and became a regular Ferrari sports car driver, later moving to the Brabham F1 team. Just as the 1977 Brabhams were coming good, Pace was killed in a light aeroplane crash.

Tony Adamowicz

Tony 'A to Z' was born in New York, and drove in American club events, progressing to TransAm, CanAm and sports cars. He won the American F5000 series and later the IMSA Championship, and was well known as the driver of Ferrari 312P and 512S sports cars, appearing at Le Mans. He is one of the few drivers to have raced both the Ferrari 512 and Porsche 917, and remains active on the vintage racing scene.

a thorough look at the cars, which at this time still consisted of M601 and M602 which had raced the previous year, and the new M603. The cars were being readied for the Daytona 24 Hours, and Bolster observed that the L72 aluminium monocoque was riveted, and had been strengthened from the original 20 gauge sheet metal in places. There were mild steel hoops in front to carry the front suspension, pedals and steering, with a steel bulkhead to support the engine as a stressed member. Upper body panels were of glass fibre, and a light-alloy tubular frame supported both the rear body section and the aerofoil over the gearbox. There were magnesium suspension uprights with front tubular wishbones. In the rear were single top links and parallel lower links, in conjunction with two long trailing radius arms on each side. The cars now used Hirschmann spherical bearings in the suspension, and Koni adjustable

The Hailwood/Watson M602 in practice at Daytona in 1973. (Courtesy Lou Galanos)

dampers. The gearbox was still the Hewland DG300, with rubber donut couplings in the tubular drive shafts, though larger roller spline shafts would be used later on. By this time the team had decided on Firestone tyres, which were fitted to the cars.

February 3-4 – Daytona 24 Hours
A four day test period at Daytona had been booked by John Wyer the week before the 24 Hours, and three cars were sent out – M601 and M602 with the DFV engine, and M603 with the Weslake engine. It had been agreed that the Weslake would only run if it showed outstanding performance in the tests. The suspect dog rings in the gearbox had been replaced, and a number of radiators were brought along for the tests. There was considerable ducting to cool the brakes, and the airfoils and fences had been refined. The DFV cars ran quite well with no major problems. Watson was quickest, the DFV car nearly two seconds faster than the Weslake machine, which had starting problems and broke

two gearboxes. John Horsman credits Howden Ganley with discovering that a number of oil pumps had been made with a machining fault which stopped the oil circulation through the coolers – an important find.

The starting problems helped Horsman to decide not to run the V12 M603, though it had a faster top speed and the engine ran very smoothly. After a number of minor modifications, the other two cars were ready for the race. The entry wasn't very impressive, as Ferrari decided it did not want to open the season with a 24 hour race and didn't like the start money, and Alfa Romeo was not ready. Thus there were the two Gulf cars, M601 for Bell and Ganley, and Hailwood and Watson were in M602. Cevert/Beltoise/Pescarolo were down to drive the single Matra MS670, and then there were a number of older Porsche 908/3s, and the new Lola T282 for Lafosse/Wisell/de Fierlant. There were also some strong-looking Porsche 911 Carreras which were expected to be good on durability.

Rain interfered with much of the practice, and at the

The Mirage coupé with the Weslake V12, in 2007. It is a shame this superb car never raced. (Courtesy Tucker Conley)

last minute the Mirage V12 was sent out to put in some laps. However, the gearbox oil became very hot and it was about to lose another box, so that was the end of the V12. John Watson got under the old Ferrari record, but Hailwood had only one flying lap before rain arrived. Eventually Bell and Ganley put M601 on pole two seconds quicker than the Matra, with Hailwood and Watson a further second slower ahead of the Lola, a Porsche 908/2 and Tony de Lorenzo's Corvette.

Bell led at the start, and seemed to be sticking to a very cautious pace, so Hailwood shot by into the lead, as did the Matra and the Lola. It turned out that Bell's engine was not running over 9000rpm, though it still held fifth and moved back up to fourth. Hailwood had a good lead, which he kept from the Matra at the first round of pit stops. When Bell came in for his stop, five minutes were lost as an alternator bracket was repaired and the clutch was adjusted. Some 75 minutes later, the Bell car was back for repairs to a broken metering unit coupling which had been causing the misfire, and the clutch was adjusted again. After four hours, Ganley, now in M601, had a clutch thrust bearing replaced, and that seemed to put that car well out of contention.

Watson had taken over from Hailwood and was leading in the other Mirage. Then Hailwood got back into M602 and was running very well until a scheduled clutch rebuild dropped him down the field. Just after midnight the

Mike Hailwood at the start in M602 alongside the Lola T282 of Wisell/Lafosse/de Fierlant. (Courtesy Lou Galanos)

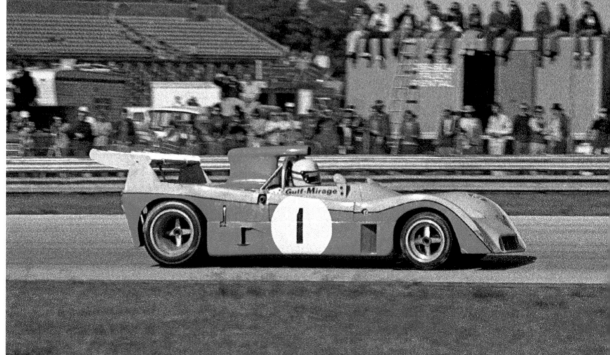

Derek Bell had M601 in the lead at Daytona, but failed to make the finish. (Courtesy Lou Galanos)

leading Matra had the engine blow, and shortly after this, the Bell/Ganley car was retired rather than do another rebuild. Then Watson and Hailwood started working to bring their car back up from the bottom of the field. Hailwood was up to 11th, when the right rear suspension broke and the body section came off, giving Hailwood a 180mph spin out of the race. This left Gregg and Haywood to press on to win in their Porsche 2.9 Carrera 911 from a 4.4 Ferrari Daytona, as all the 'stars' had gone out!

Ganley talked to the author about the race weekend:

"I had been to Daytona before as a mechanic but not driven there. Mike Hailwood and I had done the Argentine Grand Prix, and by the time we got there, Derek and Wattie had been there testing, and they had this mysterious gearbox problem. I used to have a gearbox business so John Horsman asked me what I thought was wrong. I said it wasn't getting enough oil and there wasn't enough feed to the pump, so I said this to the gearbox man and he said he had checked that and it was perfect. In the end, he hadn't checked it at all and that turned out to be the problem, down to some parts being incorrectly machined. And we were eating up clutches with problems with the thrust bearing, but the bell housing was modified and that was a great fix on John's part. He was really good on practical engineering and sorting out problems like that. One amusing thing happened at Daytona. John was out in the pit lane in the middle of the night with those aircraft signalling lights and he sees this car coming in and he waves and stops the car and it was a Matra, not a Mirage!"

John Watson was also delighted to be in the team, his first experience of a real professional and well-organised outfit:

"I had an invitation to go test at Goodwood and that came indirectly through Bernie Ecclestone. I had a good year in 1972. They had the two cars there, a Cosworth and a Weslake car, and I got into the Cosworth car and drove it sufficiently to impress John Wyer and John Horsman. The

John Wyer in typical pose during the long 24-hour race. (Courtesy Fred Lewis)

problem was that the clutch pedal would stick, and it would only happen going into St. Mary's, but that was the only problem. Then I had a run in the Weslake car which was a second and a bit slower, and overall the DFV 'package' was a better one, though the V12 had appeal as a long-distance engine, as the DFV was never intended for long-distance and 24 hour races.

"At Daytona, I settled into the car and into the team as well. It was my first time at Daytona, and I travelled there with Derek Bell who had been there before, and we got there and I looked at the thirty-three degree banking and said, 'Oh my God what am I doing here?' because when you go down the back straight into that corner it was like driving into a brick wall. I did it first in a road car flat out, and that didn't seem too bad, and then did it in the Mirage which then seemed OK. In fact, at one point, I was so impressed with my ability to go round that banking that I parked the car on the uppermost part of the banking, got out, went down the bottom and took a photograph. Then some guys came and said, 'Get that thing outta there!'"

Mike Hailwood and John Horsman ponder the numerous problems encountered at Daytona. (Courtesy Fred Lewis)

A considerable amount of effort went into the re-design of the clutch throw out bearing, moving the actuation shaft much closer to the clutch. The bell housing itself was also reinforced. This work seemed to solve the problem of repeated clutch failure.

The team booked a four-day test at Vallelunga, north of Rome, to prepare for the race there. Bell and Watson put some 1125 miles on 601, with a number of modifications being made. Watson made the quicker time, and then went out in the Weslake car. He was a second and a half slower, and after 177 miles the oil pressure went, so that was that.

Then John Watson broke his leg at the Brands Hatch Race of Champions, and Horsman contacted Australian Vern Schuppan, who had put on such a good show for BRM at Brands. The Australian had been signed by BRM at the end of 1972, but with Lauda, Regazzoni and Beltoise on the books, it was beginning to look like Vern would stay on the sidelines. Vallelunga was to be his first important sports car race.

Howden Ganley

New Zealander Ganley came to the UK in 1961, working as a race mechanic, having raced a Lotus 11 at home, and having been a race fan from a young age. He did very well in a number of formulae, especially the British F5000 Championship where he caught the eye of BRM where he landed an F1 drive. He drove at Le Mans for Matra in 1972 and then established a reputation as a first class sports car driver with the Mirage team. He also raced for March and for Frank Williams in F1, and is regularly seen at historic race events. He is also a very low handicap golfer.

John Watson

Watson was born in Northern Ireland and drove in numerous single-seater races until landing an F1 drive for Hexagon in a March 721 in 1972. He then drove a Brabham for the team, and scored a Championship point for them at Monaco in 1974. He drove for Surtees, Lotus and Penske in 1975 and finally won the Austrian Grand Prix for Penske. He then had a long association with McLaren, winning the British Grand Prix in 1981. In addition to JW, he drove in sports cars for Alfa Romeo, and stayed in sports cars until 1990.

March 25 – Vallelunga Six Hours

The entry for this race was much more impressive than that at Daytona, with Ferrari bringing three cars for Ickx/Redman, Pace/Reutemann and Schenken/Merzario. Matra had two cars with new engines for Beltoise/Cevert and Larrousse/Pescarolo, with Lola bringing an improved car for Lafosse/Wisell. GRR brought a new car, M605, for Bell and Ganley, while Schuppan was paired with Hailwood in M602.

The Mirages were at a disadvantage at the 1.9-mile Italian circuit. The cars were still too heavy, and lost time at the slow corners, and the DFV power band was very narrow, not to mention the fact that Matra had done important development work to its cars. Cevert put his car on pole in the first session, a second and a half ahead of the Ickx/Redman Ferrari. Bell could not get his Mirage within 2.5 seconds of pole, so had to settle for sixth, while Hailwood and Schuppan were seventh. The second car lost time when a driveshaft donut bolt broke, and it took 24 hours to get a replacement. M602 also had a misfire which was traced to three faulty injectors. The Wisell/Lafosse Lola T282 was a shade slower than M602, and then came the Alfa Romeo 33TT3 from Brescia Corse driven by Facetti and 'Pam.'

A large crowd came expecting a Ferrari victory, and the cheers went up when Ickx went into an immediate lead, but the groans followed as Cevert got the Matra past after six laps. The Mirages led the second group, with Hailwood's misfire having returned. Bell was in fifth by lap thirty, but Cevert had lapped Hailwood by this point, and fourteen laps later he went past Bell. The Ferraris were eating tyres, and the Matras were going a long distance on a single set. Some way into the race Cevert had his engine go, and the Ferrari fans were very happy. M605 had retired, as Ganley had been rammed by a 2-litre Chevron which had been wandering around and then shut the door on

him as he tried to fend off Redman. Some 80 laps went by while the GRR team replaced a broken rear upright, but then decided it was not worth continuing. Then Schuppan started his second stint, struggling to find gears, ending up parked on the circuit, the Hewland transmission having had a leak. GRR also suffered more damage when some of the mechanics were injured in a road crash, Alan Hearn having a badly fractured upper arm. Cevert had switched to the other Matra with Pescarolo and Larrousse to win the race by a full lap.

The Le Mans test weekend followed the Vallelunga race. GRR brought the older M601 with the Cosworth engine, and M603, now with a coupé body designed by Len Bailey, powered by the Weslake engine. This car had been in the wind tunnel at MIRA and had a lower drag coefficient than the open car, but was heavier. It took ages to get the V12 started, and when Bell drove it he felt it was down on power. It was not as fast as expected on the Mulsanne Straight, but it was really the starting issue which was the final nail in the Weslake's coffin. The decision was made to drop it and run two open, DFV-powered cars at Le Mans.

Vern Schuppan

Born in Whyalla in South Australia, he became well known after winning the 1971 Formula Atlantic Championship. This led to a test drive for BRM and a number of races, with good results in non-championship F1 events. He also drove for Ensign and Surtees in F1, but became highly respected as a sports car driver for Mirage and Porsche with whom he had a long association, winning at Le Mans in 1983. He drove in the Indy 500 three times, coming third in 1981. He won championships both in F5000 and sports cars, and won the Macau Grand Prix twice.

Derek Bell drove M603, the coupé with the Weslake engine, but it was not quick and was difficult to start. (Courtesy Hubert)

At the Le Mans test, Howden Ganley was 2nd fastest in the Mirage M601. (Courtesy Hubert)

Though unconfirmed, it seems Walter Hayes of Ford had put up the money for the Weslake engine, knowing there was a need for a good sports car engine and that DFVs would be in short supply.

Howden Ganley recalled the test weekend:

"We went over for the test weekend and that was when the team had the coupé with the Weslake engine. What I remember is that Derek, John and all the mechanics worked on trying to start the coupé and they kept most of Le Chartre awake at night trying to start it in the town centre. I was just left to play with the open car and do whatever I wanted."

As there wasn't much room in the transporter, Ganley was asked to drive M601 back to the hotel at night, and back to the circuit in the morning; something he rather enjoyed.

April 15 – Dijon 1000 Kilometers

Bell and Ganley were in M605 for the French race, with Hailwood and Schuppan assigned to M602. The couple had disappeared from the programme along with the Weslake engine, as the team concentrated on getting the best out of the DFV cars.

The Powerlok differential on M602 had been dropped for a ZF unit, and as this seemed to get the power down better, a ZF was then fitted to M605. The Matras were fastest through both pre-race testing and official practice on this new circuit, and Mike Hailwood gave the Gulf crowd a boost when he recorded third-quickest time after a series of fabulous laps, with the Mirage sliding beautifully through the sweeps. Bell was getting into the swing of things when the clutch went, worrying the team that it might not have corrected the previous problems. The engine was also changed, the new diff fitted, and Bell and Ganley were sixth. There was tension in the Ferrari camp, jolted by their performance at Vallelunga, as they were only third and fourth quickest here in Dijon.

Both Mirages had problems in the warm-up – a rear vibration managed to set the brake pads back, so the pedal went to the floor after each slow corner. The two Matras were off and gone at the start, but it was Hailwood who was holding off the Ferraris in fine style, while Bell struggled a bit with the handling. Then the Matras started having tyre problems, and the leader, Cevert, was back in sixth. On lap 29, Hailwood came in with his engine sounding flat, but it was a cracked exhaust. He was given some left-side tyres and sent off, not losing much time. As the scheduled pit stops began, Bell was leading for five laps and then came in to hand over to Ganley. This put Pescarolo and Larrousse back into a lead they would not lose. Howden then drove a very impressive stint, getting past Merzario's Ferrari and going into second place, which became first during Ferrari driver changes. Then, shortly after Bell took over, the car was back in with strange handling. A wheel bearing had gone and the wheel was wobbling dangerously, so the car was retired. Schuppan handed back to Hailwood, who was going well until he too came in complaining of handling problems. This turned out to be 'too much muck' on the tyres, so off he went with new ones. Hailwood and Schuppan ended up in fifth, behind the two Matras and two Ferraris, but again the Mirage was showing its pace and potential.

After the race, John Horsman, who had a habit of analysing everything, observed that Ganley didn't seem to use much brake pedal nor much fuel, and could have been losing a bit of time while managing that. Horsman advised him to forget all that and just " ... drive the heck out of it!" Ganley said later:

"I always thought that you had to look after a sports car, but the six hour races and even Le Mans had become like a Grand Prix, flat out all the way. John Wyer's way had been to set a time which the car could do for the whole race. But things had changed. The Ferraris were really Formula One cars, the Matra was an F1 car, and so on."

April 25 – Monza 1000 Kilometers

For the Monza race, M601 was brought back for Hailwood and Schuppan, and Bell and Ganley were now in M602. Ferrari had put in a lot of effort preparing for their home race, while the new Alfa Romeo again failed to appear. The race was to be held on a Wednesday, with practice on Monday and Tuesday. In the early laps of practice, Bell was right on Cevert's tail when the Matra engine blew up, and Bell had no vision at all. Schuppan, who had just flown back from Singapore, had to walk back to the pits when his differential gave up, after an oil union came loose. It was again looking like the Mirage would not have the pace of the Matra and Ferrari, though the car handled just as well as the opposition. Eventually Cevert/Beltoise were on pole from Ickx/Redman with Bell/Ganley sixth and Hailwood/Schuppan next.

The opening laps saw the Matra lead the Ferraris before the gap to the two Mirages, with Hailwood signalling as he passed by the team that he only had four gears. As the pit stops began, Bell was up to third, though he had not yet made his stop. Hailwood was plugging on with a difficult gearbox but holding seventh. Ganley took over from Bell, but Hailwood stayed in his car, driving very hard to make up for his gearbox problem and now an engine misfire too. At around one third distance Ganley came walking back to the pit to say his engine had gone. Hailwood had somehow managed to get the sick-sounding Mirage up to third, before Larrousse got the Matra past. Then Mike handed over to Bell instead of Schuppan, but that didn't last as the clutch broke. Ickx's pressure on the Matras worked, and Ferrari were first and second, with Larrousse/Pescarolo third.

May 6 – Spa 1000 Kilometers

The Spa race was always special, run on the 'old' 8.7-mile circuit; a blur of speed through the trees. The author made his sports car debut here, sharing Tony Goodwin's Dulon-FVC, and thus had a first-hand view of what was an amazing performance by the Gulf-Mirages. 1973 was the last year in which virtually all the F1 drivers were regularly seen in sports car races. Those present on May 6 included Pescarolo, Amon, Graham Hill, Merzario, Pace, Hans Stuck, Lauda, Ickx, Redman, Stommelen, de Adamich, as well as Bell, Ganley, Schuppan and Hailwood. Interestingly, the Grand Prix Drivers Association was actually trying to ban its members from racing at Spa, as certain drivers were adamant that it was 'too fast' and dangerous. The 3-litre

cars were now faster than the amazing 5-litre Porsche 917s of two years earlier. Beltoise and Cevert did not race, so Amon and Hill were brought into the Matra team, in spite of Matra saying it was to be only French drivers this season.

Bell and Ganley were in M605, with Hailwood/Schuppan in M602. The GRR practice session was fraught with difficulties. Lockheed brakes were tested, but then changed back to the usual Girlings, a Porsche oil valve was installed to speed up the warm-up of engine oil, the metering unit rod was redesigned and a ZF diff was used. The Lockheeds would be sorted and tried at Le Mans, and used in the cars after that race. Howden Ganley had done only a few laps after Bell's practice stint when the engine blew up. Schuppan in M602 had to be towed back to the pits when the oil pressure disappeared. Horsman decided to skip the second practice session to work on scavenge pumps and spring rates. The two cars were using quite different spring rates, but finding that stiffer springs worked much better. The author was having trouble with rearward vision in the Dulon, as the mirror fixing was not right, and

Derek Bell steers M605 through Stavelot at Spa to take the first important win for Mirage. (Courtesy Bill Wagenblatt)

Vern Schuppan shared the 2nd place M602 with Howden Ganley and Mike Hailwood. (Courtesy Bill Wagenblatt)

signalled Bell to go past on the right on the Masta Straight. Bell didn't see the signal, and moved to the left to find the Dulon doing the same thing. Bell went past at some 200mph on the grass, and we did have 'words' later, though we still remain friends!

The grid had Ickx/Redman on pole in the Ferrari, with the Pescarolo/Amon/Hill Matra next, then the Ferrari of Pace/Merzario with the Hailwood/Schuppan Mirage fourth and Bell/Ganley fifth. The new 12-cylinder Alfa Romeo would have been next, except for the fact that the author had witnessed it going into the barrier at Stavelot at high speed with de Adamich at the wheel.

The start was a seemingly disastrous one for the Mirage team. Howden Ganley recalled:

"Mike Hailwood sat on the fuel filler in his car on the grid, and all the fuel gushed up his backside and burned him. He started the race and then came in and jumped out. Horsman then asked me if I could go in that car, which was

by then dead last. I always had this ability of being able to snatch defeat from the jaws of victory! So I moved from the car that would win, to the one which was last at the time of the change over."

The start was made even worse as the Hailwood car wouldn't start (while someone was pouring milk down Mike's trousers to dilute the petrol) so the mechanics ran out and pushed it, and off Hailwood went, leaving all the Gulf mechanics to see the field bearing down on them!

Pescarolo sneaked the screaming Matra past Ickx, with an uncomfortable Hailwood right on his tail. On lap four Hailwood had a tyre burst at the Masta kink, and he limped back for Schuppan to take over, while he went off to be treated for burns. Vern then did 17 laps, and came in for the change-over. Horsman reflected that Ganley looked quite happy about this, because he felt more comfortable in a car set up by Hailwood than by Derek Bell. Ganley reported the car was now flat through Burneville and the

Howden Ganley moved from M601 into M602, after Mike Hailwood had fuel burns before the race start.
(Courtesy Bill Wagenblatt)

Masta Kink. Bell moved ahead of Amon, and moved up to sixth on lap eight. Pescarolo had tyre trouble and Ickx went into the lead. Bell was up into fourth by the 15th lap. Both the Ferraris and the Matras were making more stops than usual for tyres, and this put Bell second on lap 17, behind Redman, who had taken over from Ickx in the Ferrari. Ickx was later back in the car when the gearbox seized, so on lap 37 the Mirage went in front to the surprise of everyone. Hailwood then took over from Bell, and this pair never lost the lead. Although Ganley had managed to move from the winner to the car which would finish second, Hailwood

finished both first and second! Pace's long stop in the Ferrari saw Howden push past into second.

For the first time, the Mirages were shown an 'ease' sign, and the two cars cruised to a very deserved and much applauded win. With Hailwood's double victory, the Spa race was the very first FIA Sports Car Championship race won by the Cosworth DFV. It was also a real crowd-pleaser, and the winners had a great ovation, beating the might of Matra and Ferrari. There would not be a lot of wins like this for GRR, but this was not to be the last.

Horsman and Wyer never intended to run at the

Targa Florio, and very few prototypes showed up there anyway, and then the somewhat regretted decision to miss the Nürburgring race was also made. The official reason was shortage of engines, but in reality the team would have had difficulty getting the cars prepared for Le Mans after the ravages of the Ring, where two Ferraris led the field home.

June 9/10 – Le Mans 24 Hours

John Watson had recovered from his Brands Hatch injuries, and tested the Mirage at Goodwood before the team went to France. The new ZF 5DS25/1 transmission and Watson were tested for some 434 miles and both seemed to be fit. At Le Mans, there were the two DFV-powered cars: Bell and Ganley were in M605, and Hailwood and Watson shared M602, with Vern Schuppan as reserve driver.

The approach to Le Mans was very much standard Wyer: a 9200rpm limit in the gears and 9400 in top. The new ZF gearbox was in place, and there were plates around the differential casing to take the suspension loads. Practice was notable for a virtually total lack of excitement, with none of the teams stretching themselves for fast times. Matra was content to sit back and let Merzario/Pace and Ickx/Redman set fastest times in the Ferraris. Most time was spent on set-up and running well within limits.

John Watson had a spin, and the wind got under the tail section, lifted it, and dropped it on John's head:

"This was my first time at Le Mans, and I felt intimidated by it, which was strange as I had a penchant for road circuits. It wasn't helped by coming out of the Porsche Curve and having the bodywork come off because of the way it was located. That was a disappointment, and I didn't lose confidence but I was apprehensive. I think I got down to some half reasonable times

but I don't think they were impressive. I think having only driven the car once, and being at Le Mans for the first time and had my leg broken only three months earlier, I was cautious. I respect the circuit but I don't think the ACO kept step with safety improvements after Bonnier's accident in 1972. But you take Le Mans as it is and for what it is, and if you feel uncertain about it, then you don't drive there ... and for me it was 22 hours too long!"

Ferraris and Matras had the first seven places on the large grid, with Bell/Ganley/Schuppan next, nine seconds off pole but actually quite close to the Matra times. Then came Hailwood/Watson/Schuppan (Vern drove both cars) a second slower, but three seconds ahead of the Lola-DFV. While the Ferraris and Matras led the Mirages in the early stages, Mike Hailwood was one of the first in trouble.

Howden Ganley shared M605 at Le Mans with Derek Bell. It was essentially a st session for the team. (Courtesy R Bunyan)

He was having to change gear without a clutch from the beginning, and came in for an early stop to have it adjusted, which dropped him well back. Then after only 29 laps, Bell came in with only fourth and fifth gears, as the input shaft had stripped in the new ZF box. It took four and a quarter hours to repair this.

Horsman saw this as essentially a test to be learned from, observing that races like Le Mans provided much longer periods than any test session. The Hailwood/Watson car had been steadily moving up the field, and got into third place by the seventh hour. Then Schuppan was behind the wheel, and lost a place when a new spark box had to be fitted. Just after midnight Vern slid wide at Tertre Rouge, got sideways, and rolled the Mirage. The other car was now some four hours behind, but again was making progress until it was stopped, with Ganley at the wheel, when the left-hand bank of cylinders seized in the bores. The pump for that side of the engine was not delivering enough water at the high speed circuit, and cavitation developed, something that would not happen in a test session. So Howden was left sitting at the side of the road:

"The pump had been rebuilt, but we had been using a lot of oil, and because of the rules at Le Mans you had to

Mike Hailwood drove superbly at Le Mans. He is seen here coming through the Esses. (Courtesy Bill Wagenblatt)

carried that one around for a long time. John Wyer, however, was always pretty forgiving to his drivers who owned up to what had happened, and of course Vern remained a Mirage driver.

June 24 – Österreichring 1000 Kilometers

In the short time before the Austrian race, Horsman went to the ZF factory to sort out the input shaft failures caused by vibration from the Cosworth engine. ZF decided to decrease the diameter of the shaft to allow for the vibration, and that solved the problem. M605 for Bell and Ganley, and M602 for Hailwood and Watson were sent off to Zeltweg, where practice showed the Matras were on top form. The author was also driving there, this time in John Blanckley's Scorpion-FVA, having been summoned at the last minute by the late Brian Kreisky because the "Austrian paying driver kept getting in the wrong side of the car!"

It was extremely wet in Friday practice, but Bell took advantage of his skill and new wet Firestone tyres, to set impressive times. Then the oil pump belt broke and the pressure disappeared, so he was sent out in the other car. On Saturday, there was a short spell of rain before the sun came out. Cevert set very quick times in the Matra. Bell was pressing on, and managed to touch the Armco on the flat right-hander at the top of the hill at some 150mph – but got away with it. The Hailwood/Watson Mirage ran well in the 'warm-up' on Sunday after an engine change, while the Scorpion lost its clutch, which was still being fitted when the race started. There wasn't time to fuel up, and the author set off, only to encounter fuel pressure problems which made the touchy FVA engine cut out

do a minimum number of laps before you could add oil. John (Horsman) asked me to nurse it around until we could put some oil in, and when it stopped it was empty. Earlier on, I was on my in lap and I came around Tertre Rouge to find the other car upside down in the road. So I came in and said to John, 'There is a Mirage upside down at Tertre Rouge' and he said, 'What are you talking about?' and I thought maybe I had seen a mirage and got it wrong! Derek got in our car and drove off and John said again, 'What did you say about the other car?'"

The engine incident led to GRR welding another inlet from the radiator into the left-side water pump, something which Cosworth would later do themselves.

Vern Schuppan and the author would later share a works Ford Consul GT in the first running of the Avon Tour of Britain. Vern recalled how badly he had felt about crashing the Mirage at Le Mans. It was not until sometime later that John Horsman told him that his engine would have seized anyway, just like the Bell/Ganley car, but Vern

in the most embarrassing places, so the car was retired over the team's protests.

The two Matras quickly pulled away from the Ickx and Pace Ferraris, with the Mirages in pursuit. On lap eight, Hailwood changed into neutral on the fast corner before the pit straight, spun, and found himself face-to-face with Derek Bell, both travelling in the same direction. Hailwood told the author afterwards that he thought it was Bell going the wrong way! The Mirages were third and fourth when the pit stops began, and they were hoping to do the race on three rather than four fuel stops. The Bell/Ganley car would have taken the Ickx/Redman Ferrari for third, had Bell not been forced to make a longer stop for brake pads.

Pescarolo/Larrousse and Cevert/Beltoise took the first two places from the Ferrari, with Hailwood/Watson fourth ahead of Derek and Howden, and the Pace/Merzario Ferrari sixth. It was a race in which the Mirages demonstrated they could compete with Ferrari, but the Matras were in a class of their own.

July 21 – Watkins Glen 6 Hours
Watkins Glen sometimes has a lacklustre entry for the Six Hours, as it is the last race in a championship that has already been decided. However, this time, there was still to be another race at Kyalami, so all the teams took Watkins Glen seriously. Mirage had been doing work on the brakes,

John Watson in M604 is out-powered by the winning Matra of Gerard Larrousse. (Courtesy Bob Graham)

The Mirage team stayed on at Watkins Glen for a test session after the race. (Courtesy Tucker Conley)

switching to Lockheed from Girling. The drivers preferred Lockheeds, whereas the Girlings were favoured by the mechanics for ease of changing pads.

Some reports have the drivers in the same cars as in Austria, and others have Bell/Ganley in M602 and Hailwood/Watson in M604, which would be a new car. John Horsman's usual detail doesn't cover this in his book so it remains uncertain. Hailwood was the quickest Mirage driver in practice, a touch faster than Watson. Both cars were handicapped as the Cosworth couldn't deliver the acceleration that the 12-cylinder engines managed. Bell did most of the work in the other car, with Ganley doing relatively few laps, and they were just behind their team-mates on the grid. It was clearly going to be a case of the Matras going away from the rest, the only question being by how much.

Rain had been constant until just before the start. Only

Bell had remained on intermediates, as everyone else went for slicks. The Mirages had been much quicker in the wet than anyone else, so it was a big disappointment when the sun came out. Bell was in the pits changing back to dry tyres when the flag went down, so he was under real pressure. Hailwood hung onto the leaders, while Bell started nearly a lap in arrears, but by lap nine was all the way up to sixth. Cevert and Beltoise had been having trouble managing the early laps this season, and sure enough they drove into the back of Ickx's Ferrari, requiring major body repairs to the Matra. When Ganley took over from Bell, he had a misfire and came in for a new spark box. Hailwood had a puncture, and then severe brake pad wear. Bell, back behind the wheel, had the fuel pump stop, a result of fuel from Gulf somehow having grit in it.

When Cevert finally retired, the race positions were much like Austria, and Pescarolo/Larrousse won again from Ickx/Redman, with Pace/Merzario third, then the two Mirages. Bell was some 19 laps behind the winners, and 16 laps behind the third place car. After the race Horsman said to Ganley, "You're required on the podium, you have been judged rookie of the year." Ganley thought that, "Horsman was pulling my leg because I had raced at the Grand Prix in the previous two years."

John Watson had enjoyed his trip to upper New York State:

"I love Watkins Glen, and this was the first time I went there. It's the layout of the circuit. To me it's one of the finest race tracks of my racing life. The location and the atmosphere of the circuit both at the Grand Prix and the Six Hours are very special. Being in America in the early 1970s when England and Europe were in an appalling state politically was terrific ... just going to a shopping mall! The shame was we were trashed by the Matras, which were really on form ... the best car, great chassis, good drivers and a super operation. At Watkins Glen, you would come out of Turn One and it was almost flat up through the Esses until Turn Four, and that was just power. The Mirage was good, but it just couldn't match them on power and pace. I enjoyed being in the team. It was the first time I was in a fully professional team, and I was very much the new boy. I was the rookie

Howden Ganley is about to drive, as Derek Bell watches. Ganley had the throttle stick and had a serious accident. (Courtesy Tucker Conley)

with long hair and a beard ... not quite the image! I was slightly uncomfortable in a setting where everything was so organised and people did things for you. I wasn't used to that. I was grateful for the opportunity to drive for John Wyer, which was good for my career, at a time just when it looked like sports car racing was going into something of a decline."

The team stayed at the Glen for some testing. It was during this test that Howden Ganley had a big crash – only the second time that a Mirage driver was injured. Howden was coming through the right-hand corner before the old pits, where he would slide the back around, but the throttle stuck open due to a worn pedal pivot bearing. Howden went into the guardrail and injured his foot and toes quite severely. Johnny Rutherford was on hand to drive and he went to Ganley's aid. The stoical Ganley didn't have hospital treatment, and just put up with it according to John Horsman. Ganley recalled the incident:

"I had the throttle stick open at the corner before the pits and it just went straight into the barrier flat out. A rivet head had lifted and when the pedal push had worn down, it allowed the pedal to get down behind the rivet."

September 16 – Imola 500 Kilometers
The championship round at Buenos Aires, scheduled for the end of October, had been cancelled. GRR had been working on lightening the cars after Watkins Glen, but had not made huge progress. The team arrived at the non-championship event at Imola with one car with a lighter nose, and one with a lighter tail section. Hailwood was entered in one heat in M602, while Bell would run in the other in M601, and hopefully both would then appear in the final. The only real opposition would come from an Autodelta Alfa Romeo 33TT12, in the hands of Rolf Stommelen, which was very quick, but suffered due to the wrong choice of tyre.

GRR was doing some development work at the event, making numerous changes to aerodynamic devices, trying

26in rear tyres instead of 24in, and removing the fibreglass sills to save more weight. There were more fuel pick-up problems in practice – though that was sorted by relocating the pick-up point on the right-side tank. Bell had falling oil pressure as well as the fuel problems in practice. On the second practice day Bell's woes continued, as the engine would cut out under braking, even while gently bedding in new pads. Hailwood meanwhile had a leaking gearbox and low oil pressure, so the engine was changed. With little opposition, the Mirages were second and third-quickest behind the Alfa.

Hailwood led Heat One, but a great plume of smoke appeared after several laps, disappeared, then reappeared. All the oil had leaked from the gearbox, and it just stopped working. Heat Two looked more promising, with Bell up against Stommelen and Mario Casoni in a Lola T280-DFV. Stommelen pulled away by a second per lap, but after ten laps he was in the pits, his soft Goodyears wrecked, so new ones were fitted. Bell won the 25-lap Heat, but Casoni managed to stay on the same lap, with Stommelen getting back to third. In the final, the Alfa had to revert to harder compound tyres, so lost its 'unfair advantage'. Bell had to drive incredibly hard to stay in front of Stommelen. Towards the end of the 30 laps, the Alfa engine was a bit 'fluffy', but the Mirage handling had also suffered, and Bell's win by six seconds was warmly received by the Gulf people present.

And where were Ferrari and Matra? Matra had won the championship, and Ferrari was thinking of pulling out of sports car racing, so neither showed up.

A few weeks after the Italian race, Gulf pulled the plug on sponsorship of the McLaren USAC team, withdrawing from North American racing, though promising to continue to support the Mirage effort.

Both the Grand Prix and sports car world were shocked and saddened by the death of Francois Cevert at Watkins Glen in October 1973. He had been a superlative competitor in both arenas, and was immensely respected and liked, and his death struck a deep chord in the racing world.

November 3 – Kyalami Nine Hours

The Wyer/Horsman/Gulf/Mirage combo had enjoyed a good history at the South African race, so it was decided to send two cars out – M601 for Derek Bell and James Hunt, and M602. M602 would see Hailwood joined by endurance driver Hughes de Fierlant, who was experienced but turned out to be rather less than competitive in the team. Both cars showed up at Kyalami with the new lighter bodywork, some 200 pounds having been saved, and the bigger F1 tyres were being tried – 26in and 27in rears in both two-ply and four-ply format. The wheel arches had to be enlarged to accommodate the 27in examples, as they were rubbing the bodywork.

James Hunt, in his first endurance drive, was doing very well. Derek Bell set the car up, and James went out and was only a tenth slower. He loved the car, the first car he had driven, " ... that didn't wander all over the road." He was daunted by night driving, but remained only slightly slower than his co-driver. Hailwood was fastest of all and on pole,

---

James Hunt

Hunt started racing in Minis and rapidly moved through Formula Ford and F3, driving a March. He had an aggressive style and a number of incidents. He was dropped from the March F3 team in 1972, and was picked up by Hesketh. He won the 1975 Dutch Grand Prix for Hesketh, and the World Championship in 1976. He had a successful career with McLaren, finishing with Wolf in 1979, having been greatly affected by the death of Ronnie Peterson in 1978. He was a well-liked BBC F1 commentator. He died after a heart attack in 1993.

Hughes de Fierlant

De Fierlant was a Belgian who raced for some ten years in sports and saloon cars, mainly in endurance events. He drove a variety of cars including numerous Ferraris, scoring seven overall victories.

---

but his Belgian co-driver was four seconds off the pace. He was trying hard but just could not manage to go quicker. Jean-Louis Lafosse and Reine Wisell had the Gitanes Lola T282-DFV, and got on the front row a second slower than the Mirage. John Watson and Ian Scheckter were in a Chevron B26, one of many 2-litre cars, and Reinhold Jost and Herbie Muller shared an old Porsche 908/3.

As the flag dropped for the race start, it was John Hine from ninth place who suddenly found himself in front in the Ian Grob Chevron B23, though Hailwood and Lafosse got him before the first corner. Hine held third for a few laps, and then the Lafosse Lola was in the pits with a misfire, and out of the running. Hailwood had a lead from Bell, with Watson and Jost fighting it out behind. Then Hailwood was in with a suspected puncture – though in fact the handling was being affected by a surplus of oil on the track. Bell led until his regular stop, and James Hunt rejoined in second place. After six laps Hunt was back in with a broken wishbone mounting pin, and lost 32 minutes. De Fierlant took over from Hailwood, still in the lead, but started losing time, and then did not appear. He came in on foot and said the oil pressure had disappeared and he'd switched off. So it was now Jost in the old Porsche holding off the two litre cars.

After five and a half hours, the Porsche still led, but the Bell/Hunt Mirage had worked its way back up to second. The Mirage was catching the 908/3, but a stop for brake pads cost two laps. It was catching up again when the fuel metering unit coupling broke and a long stop meant the Porsche would win with Bell and Hunt second, some 16 laps adrift. Hunt had done a superb job and it seems a shame he didn't do more sports car races, though he did reappear in the Mirage.

1974

In theory, this book could have ended at the last chapter, as the Mirage name was retired, at least for a time, and Gulf requested that the cars now be called the Gulf GR7, rather than develop the Mirage M601 into the Mirage M701. Apparently Gulf feeling was that 'Gulf Mirage' was always shortened to 'Mirage' and they lost the publicity opportunity. Interestingly, all these years later, everyone I know refers to the 'Gulf Mirage'! For the most part, they were the same cars, though a very substantial use of titanium in many components saw the weight tumble to 1588 pounds, the lightest they had ever been, though still not down to the minimum weight. Some components had to be strengthened to deal with the Cosworth vibrations, unlike the V12 Matra, so the French team still had an advantage.

Bell and Hailwood had been confirmed as drivers in December, and news reports said the team was interested in retaining James Hunt, though John Horsman later said he was disappointed that Hunt was not quicker, and that he lacked the commitment of Bell and Hailwood. Horsman reckons that Jackie Oliver was the only F1 driver who became a sports car driver. John Wyer had been appointed president of Gulf Research Racing, since Grady Davis had retired.

A major test session was organised for the last week in February, at the Paul Ricard circuit. Though the plans for 1974 at first indicated that the team would run only one car (except for Le Mans), three cars were in fact brought for the test session. These were GR7/702, 703 and 704, which were M6/602, 603 and 604 from 1973. M6/605 had a cracked rear steel bulkhead and was made into a show car with the older, heavy bodywork and was not raced again by the team. 702 was in 24-hour spec, while 703

Derek Bell was 4th fastest at the Le Mans test weekend, in what was now known as the GR7 – this is chassis 704. (Courtesy Hubert)

and 704 were in short-race trim, and each car was quite different from the others in detail. Bell, Hailwood and Vern Schuppan drove 702 for 15 hours and encountered problems related to the DFV's vibration, but none of these would have put it out at Le Mans. The other cars also had various breakages, but it was considered a valuable test in spite of only a day and a half of dry track time. The *Autosport* report said that designer Len Bailey had altered the rear suspension to improve acceleration from slow corners, and this meant there would need to be changes from donut driveshaft couplings to constant velocity joints. A further test was carried out at Silverstone after the Ricard changes had been made, and more work was done on the '24 Hour car', GR7/702.

It was then time for the Le Mans test weekend. Bell drove 704 and Schuppan concentrated on 702, each car set up differently. Both drivers were pleased with the improvements, and 702 did 22 hours before the engine began to make odd noises. Bell was experiencing more vibrations in 704 only under conditions of high speeds or full fuel loads. This was traced to a dry cv joint, and Bell was just matching the Matra times when his DFV dropped a valve. The Alfa Romeo 33TT12 of Art Merzario was fastest of all, with Stommelen's Alfa next, the Matra of Beltoise and then the two GR7s.

April 25 – Monza 1000 Kilometers

It still seems amazing that Monza was the first race of 1974. The global oil shortage had a major impact on life around the world, and many events of all types were cancelled, shortened or changed in some way. In motor racing, Daytona and Sebring were dropped, and there was non-stop talk about making race cars more fuel efficient, which was bizarre as far more fuel was used by people driving to events than in the races themselves. And vast numbers of people in fuel inefficient cars were still attending non-motoring events.

Monza itself seemed like a trip back in time. Three Alfa Romeos headed the grid and three sets of Alfa drivers were on the podium at the end. GR7/704 was sent as the singleton entry for Bell and Hailwood, though a 'T' car was also present. The Alfas and Matras dominated the dry sessions, but when it rained, Bell in 704 and Hailwood in the T-car (GR7/703) were quickest, the downforce helping the cars get the power down earlier. And of course, there were no Ferraris.

The GR7 started from sixth on the grid. It had been raining right up until the start, when it eased off, but most of the field was on wet tyres. Ickx in one of the Alfas, and Herbie Muller in the turbo-charged Porsche both shot in to change to intermediates. Two Alfas, two Matras and Hailwood headed off in one big ball of spray. After a few laps, Ickx went back onto full wets, and Hailwood moved up to fourth though he could hardly see. Matras led briefly until Pescarolo's engine went, so Merzario was now fending off Beltoise. Hailwood gradually dropped back as the track dried out, and when Bell took over, he was soon back in with a broken sparkplug electrode. He then had a puncture, so changed to slicks. Bell had a run-in with Nanni Galli in the Abarth, and after the race some Gulf bodywork was found in the Abarth! When Beltoise retired the other Matra, it was Alfa in front. Bell rose from sixth to fourth in pursuit, but lost time when the car jumped out of gear and went off at the Parabolica. Bell did well to get back onto the same lap as the third-placed de Adamich/Facetti Alfa, eight laps behind the winning car. Sadly, Swiss Silvio Moser crashed into an abandoned car near the end of the race, and died from his injuries a few weeks later.

May 5 – Spa 1000 Kilometers

GR7/704 reverted to being the T-car at Spa, and 703 was to be raced by Bell and Hailwood, the cars coming directly to Belgium from Monza. Surprisingly, the Alfas decided not to come – a serious mistake as it turned out. They hadn't remembered that it took Matra all year in 1973 to catch up after Ferrari had won the first race. Things looked more ominous for the French team when Derek Bell put the GR7 on pole from the Ickx/Jarier Matra, with Pescarolo right behind in the second blue car. Ickx went to Matra as Alfa wasn't there and he should have been the favourite.

Mike Hailwood exits Burneville on the 'old' Spa circuit in 703. (Courtesy Bill Wagenblatt)

What road racing was all about ... Hailwood chases one of the Matras through the Masta Kink. (Courtesy Bill Wagenblatt)

It is interesting that *Autosport*'s Jeff Hutchinson had referred to the Gulf car as the Mirage in his Monza report, but had changed it to 'the Gulf' by Spa. Did someone have a word?

It was a freezing cold day for the start, and the crowd had a small field to watch. The Ickx Matra got away from Bell into the lead, with Pescarolo right on the British car's tail. It looked like it might be a good race after all, but in only three laps, Pescarolo was in with overheating, and after one more lap he retired. Then Bell was in with fuel spraying from the pressure gauge. It took a lap to repair, but this meant that Ickx could relax and not push the Matra's engine. John Lepp was surprised to find himself in second in the Chevron. Bell drove very quickly to take a minute back from Ickx, but then crunched the nose with a late braking effort. Hailwood took over but the gap remained at about a lap. In the later stages, though the fuel metering unit had gone onto full rich, Bell unlapped himself to finish second behind the Matra. This meant that the Gulf team was now leading the championship. Though many people look back and see it as a season of Matra dominance, both Gulf and Alfa Romeo remained in contention for much of the season, picking up points when one of the Matras would not finish.

Hailwood risks burning his backside again – this time on 703 before the start of the race at the Nürburgring. (Courtesy Bill Wagenblatt)

May 19 – Nürburgring 750 Kilometers

The much-loved race at the Ring was one of those to be shortened 'for the sake of world economy'! Nevertheless a good entry and a large crowd showed up for the race. Matra and Alfa Romeo had been doing some testing, and practice showed that it had helped them both.

The Gulf entourage was back to two cars to race, and regrets were expressed that there hadn't been two cars at Spa, where they might well have won. Horsman says that Bell and Hailwood had 703, while 702 was in the hands of Hunt and Schuppan. However Wimpffen has this latter pair in 701 and Bell/Hailwood in 702. In any event, it is interesting that the team was running the '24 Hour' spec car in this race. Neither car was quick in practice and both were 'tail-happy,' with James Hunt having some spins. Tyres were seen as the cause, the Firestone two-ply working well on the Alfas but not on the Gulf cars, so they were swapped to four-ply, and both cars were on row three.

Soon-to-become World Champion, James Hunt, in a rare sports car appearance. (Courtesy Bill Wagenblatt)

At the start it was Matra, Matra, Alfa, Alfa, Gulf, Gulf and Alfa. On lap three Hunt tangled with the always aggressive Facetti, and came in to change a wheel. Facetti had a habit of just coming up and pushing you! Hailwood took over from Bell in the second hour and went off on his first lap, damaging the suspension. The team couldn't repair it, so it was out. Bell did the final stint in the other car, and they pulled that up to fourth in the end. It seems that the steering column bracket broke while Vern Schuppan was driving. The mechanics repaired it with plastic ties but Hunt was said to be reluctant to drive it, so Bell hopped in, although Vern Schuppan says he didn't remember Bell ever driving that car in that race. The Jarier/Beltoise Matra won from two Alfas, giving Matra a five-point lead in the series over the tied Alfa/Gulf teams.

June 15/16 – Le Mans 24 Hours

The Gulf team decided to skip the Imola race, which went to Matra, with Larrousse winning (after which he also won the Targa Florio in a Lancia Stratos). Then it was time for Le Mans. Again, the Gulf entry was interesting as 704 was there for Bell/Hailwood and the older 701 for Schuppan and Reine Wisell. The so-called endurance car, 702, was not entered, presumably because the team had made enough

Vern Schuppan drove the long-serving 701 with Reine Wisell at Le Mans but did not finish. (Courtesy Hubert)

modifications on the other cars to make them feel reliable. Both had Series 12 DFVs and ZF 5DS25/1 transmissions, and steel exhausts to stand up to the vibration. The two cars ended up with very similar practice times. Hailwood had the distributor drive shear his rotor arm, while Vern said there was a serious vibration in his car and the oil pressure was low. CV joints were changed but the vibration was still there, so that car had a new engine as well.

Bell stayed with the lead group in the early laps, but Schuppan was already in the pits with a misfire on the second lap, found to be caused by a loose earth wire, which put him well down. Bell spent many laps running right behind the four leading Matras, while Vern was in trouble again on lap 16 when the clutch went out of adjustment and he stopped on the circuit to fix it. He got back to the pits for more repairs, but after three hours and some valiant driving back up to 12th place, a cv joint went and he was out. When the Matras began to have some problems, Bell moved into third, but then he had the same cv joint difficulties as the other car, and lost 45 minutes. He came back out in 12th place, then he and Hailwood were progressing, getting back up to fourth in spite of stops to repack the cv joint covers (which were expanding at high speed and throwing out the grease).

At 8am on Sunday morning, the car refused to start. A new solenoid took 45 minutes to fit, but again it was hard to start, with just two hours to go. Nevertheless, Bell and Hailwood just kept pushing on. In the end, Pescarolo and Larousse won in their Matra, with the Porsche Carrera Turbo of van Lennep/Muller second, the Migeault/Jabouille Matra third, and the Gulf car a good fourth.

Shortly after Le Mans, the CSI's technical committee reported on its review of the FIA championships. It was announced that from 1976 there would likely be one championship for 'Makes' and a lesser series for prototypes. Manufacturers, who always felt the CSI paid them little attention, were fairly pessimistic about a good outcome for sports car racing. Ferrari had already disappeared and there were many rumours about what other teams might, or might not, be doing in 1975.

Reine Wisell

Swede Reine Wisell burst onto the F3 scene in the 1960s about the same time as his countryman Ronnie Peterson did, and he was somewhat overshadowed by him. He went into F2 and was moved up to the Lotus F1 team after Rindt's death at the end of 1970. He had some good results, but was again overshadowed by being team-mate of the young Emerson Fittipaldi. He moved to BRM, did a few more races, and went on to drive Porsches in sports car races, winning the European GT title in 1973. He lives in Thailand.

June 30 – Österreichring 1000 Kilometers

Alfa Romeos were back in strength for the Austrian race with three cars, and Ickx returning after his one race with Matra, while Matra had two cars. Gulf brought 702 to race and 701 as the T-car. There were also several strong Porsches, including a new 2.1-litre turbocharged KMW-Porsche. GRR was trying a new and very large airbox in practice, as well as a 'bib' at the front for more downforce. The engine ran better, but the handling was worse. When they set a fast time with the smaller airbox, it was realised that the big box was disturbing the air over the rear wing. This was enlarged, but too late for a better time. Thus two Matras led three Alfas and the Gulf car on the grid.

Jarier's Matra was pulling away from Ickx when Jarier suddenly rushed into the pits on the third lap, the floor having come adrift! Ickx's Alfa then led Pescarolo, with the flying Hailwood right behind and looking very competitive, in spite of very poor driving by the slower cars, and inattentive marshals. Ickx blistered a tyre with his pace, so it was now Hailwood chasing Pescarolo, and then taking the lead when the Frenchman made his stop. Bell took over and was now pursuing Larrousse for the lead. The Gulf team was optimistic, as they thought they would have one less stop, and at the next change Hailwood was again right behind the Matra. When Bell went in for his next stint, the mechanics found there was nothing to attach the left rear

Derek Bell and Jacky Ickx scored a good 2nd at Paul Ricard. This is Bell in 702 before the start. (Courtesy Quintili)

wheel to as the studs had sheared. The change of studs took ten minutes. In the end Pescarolo and Larrousse won from the Facetti/de Adamich Alfa, and the Jarier/Beltoise Matra was only 26 seconds ahead of the Gulf car, which surely would have won with one less fuel stop were it not for their wheel problem. It was a good but disappointing race. There must have again been thoughts in the team members' minds as to how often they came very close to winning.

August 15 – Paul Ricard 1000 Kilometers

Gulf decided not to contest the Watkins Glen round, which again went to Matra. Mike Hailwood broke his leg in the German Grand Prix when his McLaren crashed, and he was out for the season. Freelancing Jacky Ickx contacted the Gulf team and was signed to join Derek Bell, while the second car was back for Schuppan and Wisell. There is a distinct feeling in John Horsman's book that the team was giving up hope of winning by this point in the season.

The Matra onslaught continued at Ricard, where they took their seventh win of the season. There were thirteen 3-litre cars in the entry, but Alfa Romeo had again decided not to come. Matra usually did most of their testing at Paul Ricard, so the cars were finely tuned to the circuit. The Gulf cars were over two seconds slower than their winter testing time in first practice, so there were immediate engine changes. Schuppan had an upright break in pre-practice testing. Times improved slightly, but analysis showed that the Matra torque range allowed them to accelerate much quicker on short straights, and the Cosworth just couldn't match this. Wisell blew an engine, and then used the training car which had clutch problems. Nevertheless, Ickx and Bell were on row one with Schuppan/Wisell behind them.

Bell and Schuppan managed to stay on terms with the Matras in the early laps of the race. As they caught slower cars, Bell got knocked off twice, and took a long time to get restarted the second time. When it came to the scheduled fuel stops, Schuppan handed over to Wisell but the starter motor jammed, just as the Bell car arrived, so chaos ensued. Wisell lost many laps while the starter was rebuilt, and after another seven laps it cut out again, so the car was retired. Ickx and Bell drove a superb race to get within a lap of the second Matra, but a locking brake put Bell off twice and they had to settle for third.

September 29 – Brands Hatch 1000 Kilometers

Autosport reported in mid-September that the Gulf team had been testing at Silverstone and Brands Hatch prior to the Brands Hatch race at the end of the month. While it is not entirely clear, it would seem that one of these cars was the new-for-1975 GR8/801, a new Len Bailey design with a wheelbase 6.1 inches longer than the GR7. It used the

Derek Bell and David Hobbs managed 3rd place at Brands Hatch in spite of many mechanical problems. (Courtesy R Bunyan)

Reine Wisell settled well into the GR7.
(Courtesy Pete Austin)

same bodywork, though the rear section was lengthened to take account of the additional 6.1 inches.

On September 22, Paul Weldon drove the ex-Anthony Hutton/Malcolm Guthrie Mirage M1 to victory in the Historic Sports Car race at Aintree.

Two unspecified GR7s ran at Brands Hatch for Bell and David Hobbs, and Schuppan/Wisell. New noses were fitted for practice to increase downforce, but these seemed to provide too much to be useful. However, in the wet session, high profile Firestones on 18in rims had Bell two seconds quicker than the Matras. In the dry, Matra set the

Vern Schuppan managed quick times at Brands Hatch in spite of the weather. (Courtesy Pete Austin)

fastest times, followed by Bell/Hobbs, and then came the new Gethin/Redman Chevron B26 ahead of the second Gulf car. The Matras led the race from the start, ahead of the Gulf GR7s and then the Chevron. On lap 16 Bell went off at South Bank, hit the barrier and stopped to repair the nose. The air duct was bent and that would lead to overheating brakes later in the race. By one fifth distance the French cars led Wisell/Schuppan, with Bell/Hobbs in eighth. At halfway, Bell was in fifth, but then the Wisell/Schuppan car retired with a driveshaft problem. Bell and Hobbs moved up to third, but the car was trailing smoke from the grease escaping yet again from the cv joints. This car was just closing on the second Matra when it required new brake pads, as a result of the overheating. It finished third, with the amazing little Chevron fourth on the same lap.

November 9 – Kyalami Six Hours

Once again, the Gulf entourage made the trek to South Africa. Driveshafts with sliding spines had been tried after Brands Hatch and were adopted for both the GR7s and the new GR8, and although inboard brakes were also tried, it was decided not to use them.

Both practice and the race were much like Brands Hatch, with Matras quickest, finishing first and then second, and the Gulf second in practice and third in the race. GR7/701 was there for Bell and Hobbs, again with a second car for Schuppan and Wisell. Vern spun, damaging the radiator and water pump, and Derek had an off-course excursion which damaged the fuel tank and nose mounting. Hobbs then drove Bell's car after it was repaired, and but a rear radius rod broke after six laps. Finally Wisell had the rear wing collapse on the second car ... all this in the first day.

On Day Two, Bell spun after only four laps when his engine blew, but his first day time gave him third on the grid. Schuppan and Wisell had lots of oversteer and a misfire in GR7/704. Autosport reported that the team didn't bring the 'modified' chassis from the Brands Hatch test – John Horsman saying that he didn't want to bring

a new car with untested parts and that " ... it was no faster than the old cars."

Beltoise made the best start, but it was Bell who slotted in behind him. It took a few laps before Larrousse got the other Matra past, and by this time Bell was already in difficulty with overheating rear tyres. Both Gulf cars had tyre trouble, Bell having a spin, and then Vern stopped when the throttle cable broke. He removed the air intake, stood on the seat and operated the throttle slides by hand to get back to the pits. The spring was so stiff he had to stop three times to rest. Bell and Hobbs managed to stay in third place, and were taking eight seconds a lap back from the Matra. The Schuppan/Wisell car had lost thirty minutes and was now limping round with oil smoke blowing out the back, and it had started raining hard. Then Schuppan did not appear, the wheel nut having fallen off, so an hour was lost while one was sent out, with Vern sitting in the pouring rain. The car got back to the pits but was too far behind to be classified. The Matras were using slick tyres but they ran smoothly to finish six laps ahead of Bell and Hobbs, with the John Lepp Chevron fourth.

M6/GR7 SPECIFICATION	
Presented	March 14, 1972
Type	Two-seater open car
Engine	Ford Cosworth DFV V8
Power	445bhp @ 10,500rpm
Capacity	2993cc
Brakes	4 ventilated, cross-drille discs
Transmission	M6-Hewland DG300; GR7-ZF 5DS25/1
Chassis	Aluminium monocoque with steel reinforcements, fibreglass reinforced polyester body
Wheels and tyres	Firestone tyres, various sizes over three years

1975

Matra finished the 1974 Championship with 140 points to the 81 for Gulf, and 78 for Porsche, so for Gulf it was not much of a reward for considerable effort. With the world economy in the doldrums, and sports car racing on the decline, Gulf decided to make drastic cuts to the programme for 1975. In fact Gulf wanted to pull out altogether, and John Wyer made huge efforts to talk them out of this plan. The decision had been made in late 1974, but Wyer argued that the sale of the GR7s and the eventual sale of the GR8s, along with a real chance of victory at Le Mans, was a far better choice then disbanding Gulf Research Racing at the end of 1974.

As Le Mans was to be run as a 'fuel efficiency' race, Wyer contended that the team would have its best chance to gain the invaluable Le Mans publicity. Of course, Matra had quit sports cars and gone to Formula One, and the only manufacturer that would be serious about the 1975 season was Ligier. At the last minute, Willy Kauhsen put in his own money to bring the 1974 Alfa team back to life as well. Gulf did not approve the Le Mans budget until May of 1975, though fortunately Wyer and Horsman had kept the work progressing with fewer staff.

The team had sold GR7/702 and GR7/704 to the German entrant/driver George Loos at the end of 1974. 703 and 705 would get sold to the United States. On March 23, one of these cars, presumed to be 704, was entered for the Mugello round of the World Manufacturers Championship, the first round having been at Daytona. There were Alpine-Renaults and Alfa Romeos present, and a number of Porsches. The car was entered as a Mirage, but in the red and yellow livery of GELO racing for Jochen Mass and Tim Schenken. It qualified quite well in fourth but exited early with an ignition problem. On April 20, Loos again entered one of the cars, once more for Mass and Schenken, in the Monza 1000 Kilometres, and it came as something of a surprise to all those there when the 'Mirage' qualified on pole – ahead of the Alfa Romeos that were sweeping the series. The car ran very well at the outset, Mass having a very lively tussle with Larrousse, who was sharing an Alpine-Renault with Jabouille. Mass led at the pit stops, and when he came in to hand over to Schenken, the battery was dead and had to be replaced. Schenken worked back up to second, and then the Alpine had problems. The Mirage was going well when the rear wing collapsed and punched a hole in the gearbox, draining the oil so it failed to finish.

June 1 – Nürburgring 1000 Kilometers

The Loos car did not appear at Spa, but Howden Ganley was in 704 with Schenken on June 1 at the Nürburgring 1000 Kilometers. 702 was also entered for John Watson and Tom Pryce, and Loos had three other entries as well.

Watson/Pryce were sixth in practice with the other car eighth. However 702 had an accident at 27 laps and was out. George Loos, perhaps not the most predictable of team managers, made a serious error when 704 was running behind the Merzario/Lafitte Alfa near the end of the race. The cars could have gone eleven laps between stops but Loos brought Ganley in at ten laps. As Ganley started to get out of the car to hand over to Schenken, Loos changed his mind and told Ganley to stay in. He then sat on his seat belts which lost time, and in the chaos the team forgot to change the hard-working front left tyre. Howden then drove the rest of the race with a near-useless tyre and couldn't catch the Alfa, which would have been possible if the management hadn't interfered. The Ganley car had been leading by 29 seconds, which turned into a 29 second deficit, so it was an unfortunate result.

Howden Ganley remembered the return to the car:

"The Gulf mechanics came to the race to look after the cars because Loos was also running Porsches. John Horsman couldn't come because he was getting the GR8 ready for Le Mans, so Len Bailey came. We very nearly won that race except for the mix-up."

June 14/15 – Le Mans 24 Hours

The GR8 chassis was constructed so that an aerodynamically efficient body could be fitted, which would be at its best on the Le Mans long Mulsanne Straight. There was no budget

Finally, the team wins at Le Mans with Bell and Ickx in GR8/801, seen here on the Mulsanne. (Courtesy Besnault)

for Bailey to design the body, so it was down to machinist Brian Holland to build a quarter scale model of the shape Horsman had in mind. Two serious problems arose: firstly the rules for the height of the roll-over bar were misinterpreted and the roof was thus higher than it should be; secondly,

Bailey, unaware that he wasn't designing the body, showed up with drawings which were co-incidentally very similar to Holland's scale model, and this caused some bad feelings. The height of the roll-over bar was set according to the height of the tallest driver, whereas other teams used

A close-up of Vern Schuppan on the way to third place with 802. (Courtesy Holocek)

John Horsman confers with Jean-Pierre Jaussaud during a routine stop. (Courtesy Besnault)

their shortest driver for scrutineering and no attention was paid after the car was approved. This meant the GR8 was taller, had a larger frontal area and more drag.

The new car was tested in February on Goodyear tyres, because Firestone had pulled out. The test took place without the new body panels. The car, with a new aerofoil, was tested with a standard DFV and Hewland gearbox, though for Le Mans there would be a de-tuned engine and the ZF box. Derek Bell tested the car again at Goodwood in April with the new body. A 'milder' engine was used to prepare for the 'fuel formula.' The cars could not refuel before twenty laps had been run, and this meant the engine needed to be more efficient than before, some 21 per cent more efficient in fact, which was something that Alfa Romeo felt it could not achieve. The engine was tuned for maximum efficiency – 8300rpm instead of 10,400rpm. The considerable effort on the body shape, interestingly, resulted in a 21.3 per cent decrease in drag, with added usable downforce. Horsman paid close attention to everything that influenced fuel consumption, in an attempt to maximise the chances of not just doing well, but winning at Le Mans. The opposition would come from Ligier, with both Cosworth and older Maserati engines, and works supported Porsches, primarily the venerable 908/3 of Jost and Casoni.

In early June, both 801 and 802 were tested at Silverstone by Derek Bell, free for Le Mans, and Jean-Pierre Jaussaud. Ickx would be paired with Bell for the race, and Jaussaud would drive with Vern Schuppan. Bell and Ickx in 801 had a good first practice day, meeting the fuel requirement test, and it was thus sent away for two full days of preparation. This was to be John Wyer's last Le Mans in a formal role and there was a tradition to uphold. Clamps had to be installed on both cars, as the rear body panels were slipping back as a result of drag from the aerofoil. 802 required a new engine after only eleven laps, but the change was efficient and the car was back for the later session to make sure it could do 21 laps on a tank of fuel. The two Gulf cars qualified quickest with the Lafosse/ Chasseuil Ligier-Cosworth next and the Jost/Casoni/Barth 908/3 fourth.

Derek Bell leads the Dorchy/Vollery
Porsche 911 RSR through the
Mulsanne Corner.
(Courtesy Besnault)

With Mr and Mrs Wyer in charge of lap timing and controlling the fuel stops, the race started, with Schuppan going out in front and the Beaumont/Lombardi 2-litre Alpine-Renault already quicker than the Ligier-Maserati of Beltoise/Jarier. But the Alpine ran out of fuel and never made it back to the pits, and in fact eight cars never made it to the twenty-lap mark. The Gulf team had cleared the fuelling procedure with the organisers, but in spite of that there were problems when the officials were deciding who would win the Index of Efficiency.

It was not an exciting race for spectators, with very little sprinting and few battles between cars – it was all about endurance and eking out the fuel. In the sixth hour, 802 started to misfire. A 25-minute stop to change the ignition box, and then a puncture dropped that car to fifth. At hour 16, Ickx came in to report a vibration, and the tyres were changed, but Bell came back in three laps to say it was still there. A lap was lost in checking everything, and Bell was then running at about 11 seconds per lap slower. With three hours to go, it started to rain so wet tyres went on, which were later switched for intermediates when it started to dry. It was at this point, on lap 312, that Ickx came in with a cracked exhaust which took 12 minutes to repair. Bell took over for the final stint, and 801 won by a lap from the Lafosse/Chasseuil Ligier, which was five laps ahead of Schuppan and Jarier. In spite of the fuel restrictions, the winning car was only one lap short of breaking the Matra's distance record of 1974, and the de-tuned engine was still managing 196mph on the Mulsanne Straight. The vibration was later traced to a lower engine mounting broken through the bolt hole. When checked, the mechanics had not seen that it was cracked.

The race had been a great success for GRR and Gulf, Horsman and Wyer ... with a bit of luck as well! The team could hardly believe they had finally got a Gulf/Mirage/GR8 to win Le Mans.

Towards the end of the season, GR7/703 had been sold to Harley Cluxton III in Arizona. Cluxton asked John Horsman to assist in running the car at the Elkhart Lake Handicap race in August, which he did. The result was that

Vern Schuppan won the race against some CanAm cars, in spite of driving the last laps in heavy rain on slicks. It was a good result for Vern and as it turned out for Horsman as well.

Jean-Pierre Jaussaud

Jaussaud started racing in 1962, and went into Formula 3, going to Matra in 1966, and winning the French F3 title in 1970. He went into F2, and was one of the toughest and best competitors in that category. He quit single-seaters in 1975 to go endurance racing, winning at Le Mans in 1978 and 1980.

On September 7, Howden Ganley drove one of the George Loos cars to second place at the Nürburgring Interseries Sprint, behind the Loos Porsche 917-10 of Tim Schenken. Ganley had done a demonstration run in the GR8 at Silverstone at the British Grand Prix – the last time the Gulf colours would be seen in Europe. On September 29, Ganley again drove a Loos GR7, this time 704 at the Hockenheim Interseries race, where he was third. Ganley was very impressed with the braking on the Mirage, and had managed to beat the Alfa Romeos. He had a good tussle at Hockenheim with Derek Bell in his Alfa, which finally ran out of brakes.

The GR8s were fully rebuilt, and M6/605 had now been made into a GR8 show car for Gulf's use, having been brought back from the United States. The Gulf Research

GR8 SPECIFICATION

Presented	February 3, 1975
Type	Two-seater open car
Engine	Ford Cosworth DFV V8 (from 1977 with Renault engine)
Power	375bhp @ 9000rpm
Capacity	2993cc
Brakes	Four internally ventilated and cross-drilled discs Transmission ZF 5DS25/1
Chassis	Aluminium monocoque with steel reinforcements, engine mounted semi stressed
Wheels and tyres	Goodyear tyres

(Note: The following M9 and M10 cars used the same chassis as the GR8, and many of the same components; DFVs were replaced with Renault engines, and then the DFV returned for 1979)

Racing Company finally closed its doors at Slough on November 30, 1975. Gulf had made a major contribution to motor racing between 1967 and 1975 and had received vast publicity. However, the Mirage race cars were not finished.

The post JW-Gulf years
1976/1977/1978 GR8-M9 – 1979 M10 – 1982 M12

1976

The GR8s and all the spare equipment had gone into storage at Maurice Gomm's workshops, as there were no takers for the rebuilt cars at the end of 1975. But in March 1976, Harley Cluxton decided to buy the cars, and asked Horsman to organise and run them at Le Mans. Anthony Bamford's JCB company would sponsor the Le Mans entry, with input from Total Oil and Goodyear, and the cars were repainted in JCB colours. A DFV with full F1 cams was rebuilt, and Horsman assembled a number of the GRR team members to assist in preparation and in running the effort at Le Mans. The drivers were to be Bell, Schuppan, Lafosse and Francois Migeault, and the cars were entered in the name of Grand Touring Cars, Cluxton's Ferrari dealership and restoration business in Arizona. Even John and Tottie Wyer would come along and do the lap charts. The cars were shaken down at Silverstone in late May before the team set off for France.

June 12/13 – Le Mans 24 Hours

Fuel regulations had been scrapped for 1976, but the race was still not a World Championship round, since the organisers had invited just about every type of closed racing car in existence – sports, Group 5, GTP, IMSA GT, GT, Touring and NASCAR!

The opposition was much tougher than in 1975, with Porsches and Alpines having more powerful engines. Bell and Schuppan in 801, the 1975 winner, had a misfire at the start of practice so the engine was changed. The Migeault/Lafosse car was fine and did little running to allow the usual careful preparation. The Alpine A442 of Jabouille/Tambay/Dolhem was fastest, and was also driven for a few laps by none other than Jackie Stewart. The Ickx/van Lennep Porsche 936 was next, followed by the Schurti/Stommelen Porsche 935, a French Lola T286, the Jost/Barth 936, then Bell/Schuppan in what was now being called a Mirage again, and then Lafosse/Migeault.

The Mirages settled into a very steady pace in the opening laps, though Bell came in on lap six with a puncture, and the rear tyres were changed. Some of the quicker cars retired before the halfway stage, including the pole-winning Alpine and the Jost/Barth Porsche. 802 ran very smoothly with nothing but routine stops until the 18 hour mark, when it lost 32 minutes after failing to restart. The electric fuel pump had to be replaced. The Bell/Schuppan car had an alternator failure at 10 hours, when the two

Francois Migeault

Migeault managed to get himself into F1 in the little Connew team, which did not last long. Then he went to BRM, the Embassy Hill team, and Williams. He also drove an Osella quite quickly in F2 races, and did Le Mans several times.

Jean-Louis Lafosse

Born in Senegal, Lafosse started in a Renault-Gordini, and moved into sports cars, of which he drove almost every make. He was very competitive in the 2-litre sports car series. A tough but very well-liked driver, he was killed at Le Mans in a Rondeau in 1981.

Mirages were third and fourth. There were several more electric problems for that car during the next 30 laps, after which it ran smoothly, behind the de Cadenet Lola. The Lafosse/Migeault 802 was in second spot near the end when the tail section fell off. Lafosse ignored signals to come in and drove slower, risking disqualification. He finally pitted for a replacement tail section, just finishing in second ahead of the Lola. Ickx and van Lennep won, the Lola was third, Schurti/Stommelen fourth, and Bell and Schuppan fifth – a very good result for Cluxton.

French drivers Lafosse and Migeault in 802 managed a worthy 2nd place with the Renault-powered Mirage GR8. (Courtesy Holocek)

The Renault engine ran smoothly and relatively economically at Le Mans. (Courtesy A Sigg)

August 22 – Mosport 200 Miles

The Canadian race was a championship round, but, from Europe, it attracted only the two Alpines, for Depailler and Jabouille, and the Porsche 936 for Ickx. There were, however, some interesting CanAm cars in the entry – a Shadow for Jackie Oliver, a McLaren M20 for George Follmer, and a non-turbo Porsche 917/10 which blew an engine and didn't start. Vern Schuppan was in Cluxton's Mirage GR801, sixth on the grid.

The engine which had misfired in practice at Le Mans was fitted to the car. The misfire was due to too much play in the distributor bearing. It was tested at Goodwood, the unit was replaced, and the Hewland box was put back into the car. In the race, Ickx stayed in contention with Oliver and Follmer, but the Group 6 cars needed to refuel so he finished third behind them, first in the championship class, with an Alpine next, and then Vern third in the class, fifth overall. Afterwards, all the Mirage equipment was sent to Arizona.

Vern Schuppan took 5th against several CanAm cars at the Mosport 200 for Harley Cluxton in GR8/802.
(Courtesy Ellwood)

801 and 802 at the start of the 1977 24 Hours, with Leclerc and Schuppan driving. (Author collection)

1977

Discussions at the Mosport race in 1976 ended with a major change for the Mirage cars. Horsman and Cluxton talked to Gerard Larrousse and an idea was proposed that the pair run Alpine-Renaults in 1977. After a trip to France by Horsman and Cluxton there was a counter-proposal that the Renault engines should be fitted in the existing Mirage GR8 chassis, and that, with help from Len Bailey and Maurice Gomm, was what happened. Renault agreed to supply four engines and a dummy engine for a show car, in exchange for $42,000 and an agreement that there be a French driver in each car at Le Mans. Again, Horsman called on many of the ex-Gulf people and the stripped chassis were sent to England for Gomm to prepare for the engines. After a press launch in late March, the race engines were installed, and 802 ran at Phoenix International Raceway on April 12, with Vern Schuppan driving. Then Vern and Sam Posey did 20 hours of endurance testing and the car seemed to be in very good shape.

June 11/12 – Le Mans 24 Hours

When the GR8 arrived for practice, the team's main issue was discovering the error made back in 1975. Back then, the dimensions for this car's roll-over bar and cockpit were based on the tallest driver rather than on a shorter driver. While this had made relatively little difference in the 1976 race, it was significant now that other cars had more power.

The increased drag, and the use of a large intake for the Renault engine lost some 90bhp, and the Goodyear tyres gave a different gearing than the Alpine's Michelins, so instead of getting 10,000rpm on the straight, the car was limited to 8900rpm. Gearing was adjusted to compensate somewhat for this handicap, but it left Posey and Leclerc in 801 11th on the grid, and Schuppan and Jarier 12th in 802. The author was fortunate to have been able to spend considerable time with this pair during practice and the race.

Jabouille and Derek Bell were on pole in the Alpine-Renault, ahead of the Lafitte/Depailler Alpine, Ickx/Pescarolo in the Porsche 936, the Tambay/Jaussaud Alpine,

Sam Posey ran out of fuel when a pump leaked, so 801 was forced to retire.
(Courtesy Legros)

103

Vern Schuppan put in many fast laps on Sunday morning in a great effort to catch the leading Porsche.
(Author collection)

and the similar car of Arnoux and Pironi. It was this car, meant to be the team 'hare,' which ignominiously caught fire on the first lap and was out. The Alpines had control of the early stages, and the Pescarolo/Ickx Porsche 936 was out after four hours. Ickx was switched to the other 936 which had suffered a long delay. In the darkness, Ickx was relentless in his efforts to catch the French cars. Then Sam Posey ran out of fuel in the number eleven Mirage in the night, the fuel pump having leaked. Vern brought the other

car in at 11pm with a broken alternator bracket. At five in the morning it was raining, but Schuppan was putting in very fast times on dry tyres. Wets went on when it rained harder, but Jarier damaged the front bodywork which had to be changed.

The author recalls waking up in the back of a Mini to see Ickx go into the lead, and the surviving Mirage move into third. When the last Alpine retired, this became second, and not much later the Porsche had a holed piston just like its team-mate. With one lap to go, Barth was in the pit with the 936, instructed to do one more lap and not to come past the flag until 4.01pm. He was still many laps ahead of the Mirage, which, although making up time, finished second, 11 laps down. The Mirage was, however, 16 laps ahead of the battle for third, with the next three cars all on the same lap. Renault was very pleased. Watching Vern and Jarier try to reduce the gap to the leader in the last hour was something to behold.

In September and October of 1977, a GR7 was entered in three CanAm races: at Sears Point and Riverside by Tony Fox Racing for Don Pike, finishing fifth and sixth, and again at Atlanta by Allan Bodoh for Pike, but it did not appear. Though its exact identity remains unconfirmed, this car was presumably M703 updated to GR7/703 – which had been sold to Cluxton in 1976 with the GR8s. It would also seem to be the car later raced in some CanAm races in 1978

by Alain de Cadenet with British Stamps sponsorship, and again at Mid-Ohio by Howden Ganley who finished fifth.

A real Mirage 'clan' developed in the Phoenix/ Tucson areas in the late 1970's with Cluxton, Stillwell (an ex-Australian racer), Horsman and Wyer living there. Bib Stillwell had bought 702.

1978
John Horsman stayed on with Harley Cluxton to put together a revised version of the GR8 for this year's Le Mans race. Though the two chassis remained (801 and 802) this model was now called the M9, in deference to a new lower body design with a reduced height rollover bar. This was tested twice by Vern Schuppan, reaching 208mph in the first test, still with the Renault engine.

June 10/11 – Le Mans 24 Hours
Vern Schuppan was teamed up with Jacques Lafitte in 802, and Posey was back in the team with Leclerc. The first four rows of the grid were filled with Alpine-Renaults and Porsches – two 936s and a 935. The Schuppan/Lafitte car qualified ninth, and the second Mirage was 12th; surrounded by a horde of private Porsche 935s.

The 1978 car was designated the M9, though it was still the GR8 with the Renault engine. Jacques Lafitte co-drove with Schuppan at Le Mans. (Courtesy A Sigg)

Posey and Leclerc were again in 801, and again had to retire.
(Courtesy Paul Kooyman)

The main Porsches were immediately in trouble, with both the Ickx and Haywood 936s coming in on the second lap. The Alpines took over, Michel Leclerc in the Mirage was fifth; but it was not to last. The the alternator overcharged and burned out the battery on lap 33 and they were out, Posey being deployed to the other car. Similar problems afflicted the other Mirage when the wiring harness was destroyed by a short, and lost 29 minutes. It continued until lap 174 when throttle linkage problems caused a 78 minute stop. Later, the gearbox required two long stops, so the car, which had been tenth, dropped way back, but eventually worked its way up to ... tenth! Pironi and Jaussaud won in the Alpine-Renault from Ickx/Wollek/Barth in one of the 936s.

1979

Horsman and Cluxton attempted to convince Renault and Gerard Larrousse to continue to supply engines, but all of the Renault effort was now going to Formula One, so it was back to the vibrating Cosworth-DFV.

A fully revised and even more aerodynamic body was designed and built, and DFV engines were prepared by John Judd. The DFV bulkheads had to be refitted to the chassis, there were wider brake callipers which were water-cooled, and there was a brake-balance bar which was driver-operated. In April, 801 was tested in Phoenix by Schuppan and the returning Derek Bell. A second test saw a misfire appear with a loss of compression – highlighting a misunderstanding in which Horsman had not specified to Judd the exact dimensions of the valve seat sizes. 802 also ran at Riverside with no problems.

June 9/10 – Le Mans 24 Hours

The cars, now entered as Ford M10s, had some unofficial practice before the qualifying started. The engines were pulling 9600rpm on the straight, some 213mph. 802 of Bell and Hobbs had an early engine change in qualifying, and 801 of Schuppan/Jaussaud ran without problems. This allowed the full two-day preparation time which the team always used to get things ready. The cars were eighth and fifth on the grid, with Haywood/Wollek on pole with a Porsche 936.

On lap 43 Jaussaud stopped on the circuit with no gears. It took ages for someone to talk him through removing a plate on the transmission, so he could then select second gear and get back to the pits. It took four hours to repair a broken selector shaft arm. In spite of this delay, the car might still have been classified – but for a second stop to replace electronic components. It was thus retired at 121 laps. Meanwhile, the other car, with Bell, Hobbs and Schuppan, was actually leading for three hours – as the Porsches were all in trouble with faulty wheels. Then a broken exhaust cost 27 minutes, and, after nine hours, Vern had the lights go out and he hit the barrier at Arnage. The repairs took almost an hour, and then it happened again to Bell. It then rained, more electrics were changed, the lights stopped once again, and the exhaust broke a second time. Just before the end, with no compression, the car just managed to restart, but only made it to the end of the pit

This new M10 was basically GR8/801 with a new body, and with the Ford Cosworth DFV back in place. (Courtesy Ferret Fotographics)

After hours of repairs, 801 with Hobbs/Schuppan/Jaussaud had to retire. (Courtesy Hubert)

Vern Schuppan drove both 801 and 802 at Le Mans, and is seen here being helped into the car by Jaussaud.
(Courtesy Peter/Rupert Lowes)

lane, and therefore was not classified. After all the GR8s had done at Le Mans, it was a sad ending.

1982

Harley Cluxton decided in 1981 that he wanted to have another try at Le Mans. Group C with no engine restrictions had come into being, though this meant strict controls on body dimensions. Cluxton got John Horsman to work on the new project, having spent some of 1981 with Vern Schuppan's Indy effort, where Vern was rewarded with third place in his own car. Howden Ganley was building

customer racing cars at Tiga, and agreed to build a chassis and suspension, with Horsman doing the body – all to be powered by the Cosworth 3.9-litre DFL engine. This was to be the new M12 Mirage.

Ganley explained how his involvement came about:

"I went to Indy the year Vern was third and as a result of that was asked to design and build a Group C Mirage. After some negotiation I agreed that we would do that. I basically worked out the concept of the car and the detailing was done by a young lad ... Mike Coughlan who ended up as chief designer at McLaren. We agreed that we would build the complete car which would have the 3.9 turbo DFL. Partway through the programme, there was a delay with the engine which was then delivered to us. We built everything including the roll-cage, the venturis, the lower half, the side panels, and the whole top skin was done by John (Horsman) in Arizona. To everyone's amazement we built the first car and shipped it and wondered if the two were going to match. It was absolutely spot on. I went to the wind tunnel at Lockheed Aviation with John Horsman and then built the second car, and a third chassis. And then there have been no more Mirages.

"It was an unfortunate thing. What I had wanted to do was have oil/water intercoolers. I put a big one in a side-pod, and in hindsight I should have put a small one on each side rather than one big one. The team wasn't keen on it and when they tested, I think Mario Andretti didn't like the fact that it generated heat inside the car, so they removed it. So they put their own on and went through scrutineering."

After a great deal of work the car was wind tunnel tested in March 1982, and driven for the first time in April at Riverside by Mario and Michael Andretti. There were overheating and fuel pressure problems, and the car was tested again in May with much sorting being done. There was a further test in Ohio with John Morton assisting, the car achieving 212mph. He would have driven a second car had there been time to build one.

Mario Andretti and Michael Andretti speak to John Wyer before the 1982 effort was 'sabotaged.'
(Courtesy Peter Hoffman)

The Andrettis enjoyed driving the Mirage M12, seen here on the Mulsanne Straight in practice. (Courtesy Peter Hoffman)

June 19/20 – Le Mans 24 Hours

The new Mirage M12 appeared for scrutineering, and though there were some arguments over the underside of the chassis, and the Horsman windscreen, the car was passed by the scrutineers with no other problems, so it was on to practice. Howden stated later that he felt " ... there had been a trap laid for them."

Porsches and Lancias dominated the front of the grid, with the Andrettis in a quite reasonable ninth. Stiffer springs had been fitted to deal with the downforce being generated. The clutch caused some minor problems in the race day warm-up, but was sorted. About an hour and a half before the race, a man came up to Horsman with a page from the FIA rulebook, and asked which were the oil and water coolers for the car. Half an hour later Horsman was summoned to the stewards, to be told that the oil coolers were illegally positioned and unsafe. He asked why this had not been pointed out at scrutineering, and was told

The end of the Mirage. The M10 gets pushed away after officials ordered it removed from the grid ... a very sad ending. (Courtesy Peter Hoffman)

only items of safety were inspected there. And why was the team now being penalised 'on the grounds of safety'? The committee said it would discuss it, and it was not until Mario was strapped in the car just before the start that officials came and pulled him out. That was the end of Mirage at Le Mans and in international racing. Horsman accepted the blame for not getting the oil cooler in the right place, but nevertheless, it had been missed by the ACO scrutineers. It seems very likely that someone with a vested interest had tipped them off. Horsman said it was one of the worst days of his life.

A day in the life

Fortunately, a number of Mirage cars survived the ravages of professional sports car racing, and as mentioned previously, a few of them raced in the late 1970s, and even into the 1980s. With the popularity of historic racing, and a number of championships for these machines – such as the Classic Endurance Championship – several cars have been restored and can been seen today in Europe and the USA.

The car you see in these photos has been mentioned many times in this book. It is the first of the John Wyer/John Horsman Mirage M6 cars, later upgraded to GR7 format, before becoming chassis M6/601, and finally GR7/701. It has a stunning history, and still races in historic sports car events in the hands of its Belgian owner, Marc Devis, who kindly allowed the author to test the car at Silverstone. This was a particularly significant occasion as Vern Schuppan came along to share in the driving reunion, and he was also reunited with one of the original Macon Formula Ford cars he raced, now owned by Peter Alexander.

M601 was tested extensively by Derek Bell prior to the start of the 1972 season. It ran as a team car through 1972-73-74, scoring the most points of all the team cars, covering a distance of 15,567 miles driven by Bell, Schuppan, Jacky Ickx, David Hobbs, Carlos Reutemann, Gijs van Lennep, James Hunt, Howden Ganley, John Watson and Tony Adamowicz.

The car was restored in the USA in 2003 under the ownership of Jeff Lewis, who used the car only occasionally after the completion of the restoration. In 2006 it was bought by Marc Devis and prepared in the UK by Pearson Engineering. It was brought to Silverstone for our test by Gary Pearson.

Driving M6/601-GR7/701

It is always very special to drive a well-known racing car – even more so when it is not only a car you saw in period, but raced against too. And finally, there was the chance to run the car with one of its successful drivers from the 1970s, in this case – Vern Schuppan.

On that memorable day at Silverstone the soon-to-be-announced Gulf Collection was present – six cars which had gained fame in the blue and orange colours of Gulf, including the Porsche 917, so the Mirage was a star attraction

Of course it fired on the button, the Cosworth-DFV bursting into life and causing lots of fingers to be pushed into ears! With a caution not to ride the clutch and to go easy on the intermediate tyres, it was off to do some laps around the Silverstone Grand Prix circuit.

There is little to compare, in sports car terms, with driving something which excelled on fast circuits in period, and is still very much at home in a modern high-speed venue. Though there was just a hint of a miss at low speeds, the DFV warmed to the task, the Hewland 5-speed box very much up to the job as always. The Mirage had numerous aerodynamic improvements over the years it raced, and grip and roadholding is as good now as it was in 1973, when it impressed all the other major teams. Wanting to preserve the rubber, there was no hard acceleration out of Silverstone's variety of corners, all the speed necessary coming in a straight line. A powerful feeling comes with looking down the long Hanger Straight, then finding yourself at the end of it, and working out just how much you want to ease up before turning into Stowe. The hairs go up on the back of your neck.

Vern did his laps, and like the old days, we retired to discuss laps, corners, revs, and those superb moments when Gulf, Wyer, Horsman and Mirage were at the front. Thanks to Vern, Marc, and Gary for that.

History

1972 (chassis M6/601)

Date	Event	Driver	Category	Car No	Result
14/3	Silverstone	Bell	First test		
17/3	Goodwood	Bell	Tests		
25/3	Sebring 12 Hrs	Bell/vanLennep	Race	7	DNF
12/4	Goodwood	Bell	Cooling tests		
16/4	Brands Hatch	Bell/van Lennep	Race	5	DNF
19/4	Goodwood	Bell	Cooling tests		
28/4	Goodwood	van Lennep	Tyre Test		
17/5	Nürburgring	Bell	Testing		
7/5	Spa 1000km	Bell/van Lennep	Race	7	4th
28/5	Nürburgring 1000km	Bell/van Lennep	Race	8	2nd qualf 4th race
20/6	Zeltweg	van Lennep/Adamowicz	Testing		
22/7	Watkins Glen 6 Hrs	van Lennep/Adamowicz	Race	20	12th
24/8	Goodwood	Bell	Cooling tests		
13/9	Goodwood	Bell/Ganley	Tyre test		
28/9	Goodwood	Bell/Ganley	Testing		
2/10	Goodwood	Bell/Reutemann	Brake test		
20/10	Goodwood	Bell	Brake/Tyre test		
26/10	Goodwood	Bell	Testing		
14/11	Silverstone	Bell/Ganley	DFV v Weslake		
23/11	Silverstone	Ganley/Mueller	Testing		
5/12	Silverstone	de Fierlant/Ganley	Testing		

1973

Date	Event	Driver	Category	Car No	Result
23/1	Daytona	Bell/Watson	Testing		
3/2	Daytona	Bell/Ganley	24 hr race	1	DNF
22/2	Vallelunga	Bell/Watson	Testing		
31/3	Le Mans	Ganley	Test weekend	52	
25/4	Monza 1000km	Bell/Ganley	1000km race	4	DNF

Date	Event	Driver	Category	Car No	Result
30/5	Goodwood	Watson	Testing ZF Transm		
16/9	Imola 500km	Bell	500km race	5	1st
27/9	Snetterton	Bell	Tyre test		
3/11	Kyalami	Bell/Hunt	9 hr race	5	2nd
	1974 (chassis GR7/701)				
15/6	Le Mans	Schuppan/Wisell	24 hr race	12	
30/6	Zeltweg	Bell/Hailwood	1000km race	4 'T' Car	
15/8	Ricard	Bell/Ickx	1000km race	7	3rd
6/9	Silverstone	Wisell	Testing		
11/9	Brands	Schuppan/Bell	Testing		
29/9	Brands	Bell/Hobbs	1000km race	3	3rd
9/11	Kyalami	Bell/Hobbs	6 hr race	3	3rd

M601 leads one of the works Ferraris at Watkins Glen in 1972. (Courtesy R Forster)

Derek Bell in M601 alongside Cevert's Matra at the start of the 1973 Daytona 24 Hours. (Courtesy Lou Galanos)

M601 in GR7 format at Silverstone for our test. (Courtesy Pete Austin)

The 'busy' cockpit of a period long-distance sports car.
(Courtesy Pete Austin)

The author gets in a quick lap at Silverstone.
(Courtesy Peter Collins)

The author discovers why the drivers of the period thought the Mirage had such a good chassis.
(Courtesy Peter Collins)

Handling was smooth with plenty of grip from the intermediate tyres. (Courtesy Peter Collins)

The author (left) with Peter Alexander of Macon Cars who brought along a Macon Formula Ford for Vern to try, and Vern Schuppan (right). (Courtesy Mike Jiggle)

Vern Schuppan was reunited with M601 some 38 years after he first drove it. (Courtesy Peter Collins)

Appendix
List of races

Date	Event	Drivers	Model	Chassis no	Race no	Result
1967						
25/4	Monza 1000	Piper/Thompson	M1	M10002	5	9th
		Ickx/Rees	M1	M10001	6	DNF
1/5	Spa 1000	Ickx/Thompson	M1	M10003	6	1st
		Piper/Thompson	M1	M10001	7	7th
28/5	Nürburgring 1000	Ickx/Attwood	M1	M10001	6	DNF
		Piper/Thompson	M1	M10002	5	DNS (destroyed)
10-11/6	Le Mans 24 Hrs	Piper/Thompson	M1	M10001	14	DNF
		Ickx/Muir	M1	M10003	15	DNF
	Test Weekend	Attwood	M1	M10001	12	6th fastest
		Piper	M1	M10003	14	8th fastest
10/7	Brands Hatch 6 Hrs	Rodriguez/Thompson	M1	M10003	3	DNF
13/8	Karlskoga	Bonnier	M1	M10001	2	2nd
		Ickx	M1	M10003	1	1st
23/9	Skarpnäck	Bonnier	M1	M10001	2	1st
		Hawkins	M1	M10003	1	2nd
15/10	Montlhéry	Ickx/Hawkins	M1	M10003	3	1st
4/11	Kyalami	Ickx/Redman	M1	M10001	4	1st
1968						
9/11	Kyalami	Ickx/Hobbs	M1	M10001	1	1st
23/11	Killarney	Hailwood/Hobbs	M1	M10001	2	2nd
1/12	Bulawayo	Guthrie	M1	M10001	86	1st
8/12	Lourenco Marques	Guthrie/Hailwood	M1	M10001	1	1st
26/12	Pietermaritzburg	Guthrie/Hailwood	M1	M10001	1	2nd
4/1	East London	Guthrie/Hailwood	M1	M10001		DNS gearbox

Date	Event	Drivers	Model	Chassis no	Race no	Result
1969						
13/4	Brands Hatch	Ickx/Oliver	M2	M2/300/002	51	DNF
11/5	Spa 1000	Hobbs/Hailwood	M2	M2/300/003	2	7th
		Ickx/Oliver	M2	M2/300/002	1	DNF
1/6	Nürburgring 1000	Hobbs/Hailwood	M2	M2/300/003	9	DNF
		Ickx/Oliver	M2	M3/300/301	8	DNF
29/6	Nuremberg 200	Hailwood	M1	M10001 (non-works)	6	12th
12/7	Watkins Glen 6 Hrs	Ickx/Oliver	M3	M3/300/001/301	5	DNF
13/6	Solituderennen, Hockenheim	Nelson	M1	M10001 (non-works)		DNF
10/8	Österreichring 1000	Ickx/Oliver	M3	M3/300/001/301	9	DNF
14/9	Imola 500km	Ickx	M3	M3/300/001/301		1st
8/11	Kyalami 9 Hrs	Hailwood/Gethin	M1	M10001 (non-works)	3	DNF
22/11	Cape Town 3 Hrs	Hailwood/Gethin	M1	M10001 (non-works)	3	DNF
5/12	Lourenco Marques 3 Hrs	Attwood	M1	M10001 (non-works)	3	3rd
13/12	Bulawayo 3 Hrs	Hailwood/Guthrie	M1	M10001 (non-works)	3	DNS
27/12	Pietermaritzburg 3 Hrs	Hailwood/Guthrie	M1	M10001 (non-works)	3	NC
1972						
25/3	Sebring 12 Hrs	Bell/van Lennep	M6	M601	7	DNF
16/4	Brands Hatch 1000	Bell/van Lennep	M6	M601	5	NC
7/5	Spa 1000	Bell/van Lennep	M6	M601	7	4th
28/5	Nürburgring 1000	Bell/van Lennep	M6	M601	8	4th NRF
25/6	Österreichring 1000	Bell/van Lennep	M6	M602	7	DNF
		Adamowicz	M6	M601	7T	DNS
22/7	Watkins Glen 6 Hrs	Bell/Pace	M6	M602	10	3rd
		van Lennep/Adamowicz	M6	M601	20	NRF
1973						
3-4/2	Daytona 24 Hrs	Hailwood/Watson	M6	M602	2	DNF
		Bell/Ganley	M6	M601	1	DNF
25/3	Vallelunga 6 Hrs	Hailwood/Schuppan	M6	M602	7	NRF
		Bell/Ganley	M6	M605	6	DNF
15/4	Dijon 1000	Hailwood/Schuppan	M6	M602	5	5th
		Bell/Ganley	M6	M605	6	DNF
25/4	Monza 1000	Bell/Ganley	M6	M601	4	DNF

Date	Event	Drivers	Model	Chassis no	Race no	Result
25/4	Monza 1000	Hailwood/Schuppan	M6	M602	5	DNF
6/5	Spa 1000	Bell/Hailwood	M6	M605	5	1st
		Ganley/Hailwood /Schuppan	M6	M602	6	2nd
9-10/6	Le Mans 24 Hrs	Bell/Ganley	M6	M605	8	DNF
		Hailwood/Watson /Schuppan	M6	M602	9	DNF
	Test Weekend	Ganley	M6	M601	52	2nd fastest
		Bell	M6	M603	51	3rd fastest
24/6	Österreichring 1000	Hailwood/Watson	M6	M602	6	4th
		Bell/Ganley	M6	M605	5	5th
21/7	Watkins Glen 6 Hrs	Bell/Ganley	M6	M602	1	4th
		Hailwood/Watson	M6	M604	2	5th
16/9	Imola 500km	Bell	M6	M601		1st in heat 1st in final
		Hailwood	M6	M602		DNF in heat DNS in final
3/11	Kyalami 9 Hrs	Bell/Hunt	M6	M601		2nd
		Hailwood/de Fierlant	M6	M602		DNF
1974						
25/4	Monza 1000	Bell/Hailwood	GR7	704	7	4th
5/5	Spa 1000	Bell/Hailwood	GR7	703	5	2nd
		Bell/Hailwood	GR7	704	5T	DNS
19/5	Nürburgring 1000	Hunt/Schuppan/Bell	GR7	702	7	4th
		Bell/Hailwood	GR7	703	6	DNF
15-16/6	Le Mans 24 Hrs	Bell/Hailwood	GR7	704	11	4th
		Schuppan/Wisell	GR7	701	12	DNF
	Test Weekend	Bell	GR7	704	104	4th fastest
		Schuppan	GR7	702	103	5th fastest
30/6	Österreichring 1000	Bell/Hailwood	GR7	702	4	4th
15/8	Paul Ricard 750	Bell/Ickx	GR7	702	7	3rd
		Schuppan/Wisell	GR7	704	8	DNF
29/9	Brands Hatch 1000	Bell/Hobbs	GR7		3	3rd
		Schuppan/Wisell	GR7		4	DNF
9/11	Kyalami 6 Hrs	Bell/Hobbs	GR7	701	3	3rd

Date	Event	Drivers	Model	Chassis no	Race no	Result
9/11	Kyalami 6 Hrs	Schuppan/Wisell	GR7	704	4	NC
1975						
23/3	Mugello	Mass/Schenken	GR7	704 (Loos car)	14	DNF
20/4	Monza 1000	Mass/Schenken	GR7	(Loos car)	8	NRF
1/6	Nürburgring 1000	Ganley/Schenken	GR7	704 (Loos car)	4	2nd
		Watson/Pryce	GR7	702 (Loos car)	5	DNF
14-15/6	Le Mans 24 Hrs	Bell/Ickx	GR8	801	11	1st
		Schuppan/Jaussaud	GR8	802	10	3rd
24/8	Elkhart Lake	Schuppan	GR7	703 (Cluxton car)		1st
7/9	Nürburgring Interseries	Ganley	GR7	(Loos car)	24	2nd
28/9	Hockenhein Interseries	Ganley	GR7	704 (Loos car)		3rd
1976						
12-13/6	Le Mans 24 Hrs	Lafosse/Migeault	GR8	802	10	2nd
		Bell/Schuppan	GR8	801	11	5th
22/8	Mosport 200	Schuppan	GR8	801	11	5th
1977						
11-12/6	Le Mans 24 Hrs	Schuppan/Jarier	GR8	802	10	2nd
		Posey/Leclerc	GR8	801	11	DNF
1978						
10-11/6	Le Mans 24 Hrs	Schuppan/Lafitte /Posey	GR8/M9	802	10	10th
		Leclerc/Posey	GR8/M9	801	11	DNF
1979						
9-10/6	Le Mans 24 Hrs	Bell/Hobbs/Schuppan	M10	801	11	NRF
		Schuppan/Hobbs /Jaussaud	M1	802	10	DNF
1982						
19-20/6	Le Mans 24 Hrs	Andretti/Andretti	M12	Tiga	27	DNS/DISQ

Bibliography

Books

Horsman, J – *Racing in the Rain* David Bull Publishing Arizona, USA 2006

Spain, R – *GT40: An Individual Account and Race Record*, Motorbooks International, USA 2003

Walton, J – *Racing Mechanic: Ermanno Cuoghi*, Osprey London 1980

Wimpffen, J –*Time and Two Seats – Five Decades of Long-Distance Racing*, Motorsport Research Group Washington, USA 1999

Wyer, J –*The Certain Sound*, Automobile Year Lausanne, Switzerland 1981

Journals

Autosport

Motorsport

Also from Veloce Publishing ...

The definitive racing and development history of one of Britain's most important sports racing cars. Includes international competition history & completely revised individual chassis histories of T70, T160 & T165.

ISBN: 978-1-787110-51-9

• 192 pages • 220 pictures

For more info on Veloce titles, visit our website at www.veloce.co.uk • email: info@veloce.co.uk •
Tel: +44(0)1305 260068

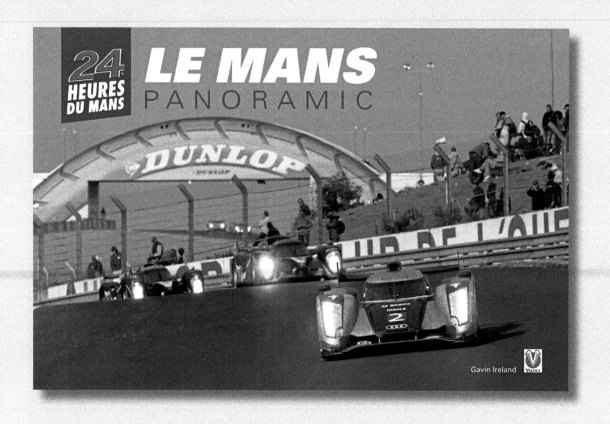

The Le Mans 24 Hours is the ultimate endurance race. This book captures the sheer scale and drama of this legendary event as never before, using specialist panoramic photography to give an unprecedented inside view of how the race is entered, watched, won, and lost.

ISBN: 978-1-845842-43-7
Hardback • 20x30cm • 224 pages • 118 colour pictures

For more info on Veloce titles, visit our website at www.veloce.co.uk • email: info@veloce.co.uk •
Tel: +44(0)1305 260068

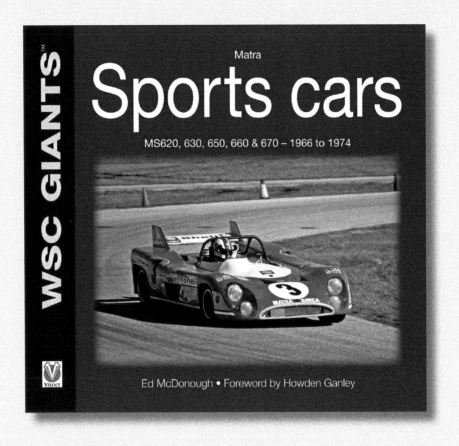

Designed and built in the late '60s by a French firm with no history of sports car racing, Matra sports cars came to dominate one of the great eras in racing, when all the Grand Prix drivers were fully active in sports cars as well as F1 machines. Includes the developmental and race history, with a full list of all events and individual chassis numbers.

ISBN: 978-1-845842-61-1
Paperback • 19.5x21cm • 128 pages • 106 colour and b&w pictures

For more info on Veloce titles, visit our website at www.veloce.co.uk • email: info@veloce.co.uk
• Tel: +44(0)1305 260068

Index